VELOCITY 2.0

PAINT, PIXELS & PROFITABILITY

Dale Pollak

New Year Publishing LLC
Danville, California

Velocity 2.0
Paint, Pixels & Profitability

by Dale Pollak

© 2010 by New Year Publishing, LLC
144 Diablo Ranch Ct.
Danville, CA 94506 USA
http://www.newyearpublishing.com

ISBN 978-0-9671565-9-0
Library of Congress Control Number: 2009937598

On August 20, 2009, I lost the person
that was responsible for teaching me
to believe in myself. Eloise Gentry, my
friend, mentor, and teacher passed away
and left behind an amazing legacy of
service to her community. Miss Gentry
taught me and others never to give up
and to always accept the challenge to
learn. This book and the learning that it
embodies is dedicated to the memory and
work of our beloved Eloise.

CONTENTS

ACKNOWLEDGEMENTS

Many people don't have the opportunity to author one book, much less two. It is with profound wonderment that I find myself once again in the enviable position of thanking people for helping bring a book to life, this time, *Velocity 2.0: Paint, Pixels, & Profitability.*

When I wrote my first book, *Velocity: From the Front Line to the Bottom Line,* many things were very different from how they are today. My youngest son Samson is now old enough to help me select the title for my book. My older sons, Austin and Alex, are both off to college. My company, vAuto, Inc., which had only a handful of employees and several hundred customers, is now the leading provider of used vehicle software in the United States with well over 2,500 customers. Perhaps the most profound change is within the automobile industry itself, having undergone transformations that are beyond simple definition.

However, the more things change, the more things stay the same. Once again I owe tremendous thanks to Lance Helgeson, my ears, eyes, and sounding board. I again want to thank my family for their support and love with a special thanks to my father, Len Pollak, for his guidance during these challenging times.

I would also like to thank all my friends at vAuto, notably Keith Jezek, President and CEO, Michael Chiovari, Chief Technology Officer, John Griffin, Vice President of Performance Management, David Hawkins, Vice President of R&D, Jill Tyson, Vice President of Finance, Morrie Eisenberg, Vice President of Corporate Development, and my incredibly hard-working and ever-smiling assistant Susan Taft. The passion, creativity, and dedication of this team is truly remarkable.

I would like to thank all of our customers and industry associates, many of whom I am fortunate to count as friends, and many of whom were essential to the writing of these pages. It is a testament to our industry that so many of us are still committed despite the enormous challenges we have faced and will continue to face.

Finally, it is with the greatest love and devotion that I acknowledge and thank my wife Nancy, who has pored over these pages for countless hours, doing what no other person could or would, for me.

Introduction: A New Day Requires a New Way

This book was written to help dealers and used vehicle managers who aspire to do a better job managing their used vehicle operations. I hope it will provide a window to examine why today's marketplace is far more challenging than ever, and highlight the new tools, technology, and best practices that a growing number of dealers and used vehicle managers are deploying to achieve success.

The name "Velocity 2.0: Paint, Pixels, & Profitability" was chosen to address the "one foot in the past, one foot in the future" nature of today's used vehicle marketplace.

"Paint" accounts for the spot-on instincts that have traditionally defined a good used vehicle manager. Every dealership needs someone who can tell which vehicles are right for their store and ensure that they stand tall. But, as you'll read in the book, I believe the instincts and skills that we've rewarded handsomely in the past need to evolve to meet the needs of a changed marketplace. This evolution requires going beyond instincts and relying on new metrics and data to manage the "paint" part of our business. Without this evolution, used vehicle managers and their dealers will achieve only sub-par success.

"Pixels," meanwhile, represents the new set of skills that dealers and used vehicle managers must understand, develop, and deploy to have a realistic shot at capturing today's Internet-enabled buyers. Today's customers start their used vehicle shopping online and what they find there defines and drives where they'll take their business. In some ways, this ever-increasing online buying dynamic has made dealers' online inventory presentation more important than their physical front line. The book will examine how some dealers and used vehicle managers have successfully embraced this trend and navigated the myriad of third-party players to craft a recipe for success. You'll also see how these efforts have transformed many of their in-store processes for managing both used vehicle inventory and customers.

"Profitability" remains the essential objective of dealership operations. In light of the dramatic changes in the environment, and the new, more varied and complex tasks that are required, dealerships must reconsider how best to structure their organizations to achieve optimal results. This subject is carefully discussed in the later chapters.

There are key themes in this book that are well known in the financial industry, but provide a new way of looking at the used car industry. These themes provide the foundation for this new way forward:

> **Volatility:** Economists call a marketplace volatile when there are significant swings up and down in the value of a given product or commodity. This definition fits our used vehicle business like a glove. With our uncertain economy, factory financial difficulties, and a greater degree of competition among franchised and independent dealers for used vehicle buyers, the valuation of used vehicles can seem like a crapshoot. It's this volatility that has spurred the leading wholesale value publishers like Kelley Blue Book and Black Book to begin publishing their benchmarks more frequently and NADA to finalize plans to launch weekly auction value updates.

> **Upshot:** Pretty much everyone recognizes that wholesale values are fluctuating faster than ever before. They recognize that wholesale values are

changing faster than monthly or even weekly. Volatility is also the reason why leasing has lost its luster. The smart money people recognize the inherent risk of trying to predict the future value of vehicles in this more volatile market. This book will detail how a new approach to managing used vehicle operations helps to mitigate some of the volatility-driven risks.

Efficiency: Financial types use this term to describe a marketplace in which buyers and sellers have roughly equal knowledge. In these markets (think of metals, grain, oil), the price of a product or commodity is largely governed by supply, demand, and price sensitivity. I believe our new vehicle business has long been an efficient market. The same is now true for used vehicles, thanks in large part to the Internet. Customers can easily find vehicles and make quick comparisons on price, features, trim packages, and financing options. The old "you can't find another vehicle like this one" line rings increasingly hollow for today's buyers. These new realities, in turn, require that dealers and used vehicle managers be more efficient and sophisticated about how they purchase, price, and present their vehicles. This book will examine the critical, often painful, steps a growing number of stores are taking to become more efficient and profitable used vehicle retailers.

Metrics-based management: The realities of a volatile, efficient market require that dealers and used vehicle managers take utmost advantage of the tools and technology available to improve the proficiency and profitability of their used vehicle operations. This book will delve into what I believe are the most critical, data-based management benchmarks to guide used vehicle decision-making and reduce the risks inherent in today's used vehicle market. I'll share first-hand examples of how dealers and used vehicle managers use these metrics to light a pathway for success.

Used vehicle primacy: You may have picked up this book because you're looking for fresh ideas and perspectives to help you manage your used vehicle operations more effectively. Make no mistake: The road ahead is not easy, especially if you consider yourself "a new car store." The success you seek will not come without making your used vehicle department a primary focus of your time and energy. The good news: This book reveals how to get there and reap the rewards of increased volumes, growth in net profits, and improved cash flow. The bad news: It takes tremendous fortitude and committed, hands-on leadership to make this important cultural transition happen. Anything less than this level of commitment invites failure.

As with my first book, I will not pull any punches in the pages that follow. If I come across as too forceful at times, I ask that you pardon my passion for our business and for what I truly believe is a fresh path that will help our industry.

Our industry is at a critical crossroads. We all need to rethink and retool the processes and approaches we have long relied on to manage used vehicle operations at dealerships. It's not that these processes and approaches are bad in and of themselves. Rather, I believe today's marketplace has rendered them largely obsolete and ineffective. As a growing number of dealerships focus on used vehicles for sustenance and, in some cases, salvation, the time is right to suggest a new way forward for our industry.

Thank you for the opportunity to share this important and transformative story.

Enjoy the read.

A NEW WAY FORWARD FOR A CHANGED BUSINESS

John Chalfant has a secret.

John is the architect behind a fast-paced turn-around in used vehicle sales at Edmark Superstore, Nampa, Idaho. In five short months, he's cranked volume to 300-plus units per month. He's turning his 400-car inventory 17 times a year. I'm paying him a visit to find out how he does it.

"So what's your secret?" I ask.

"I'm happy to talk broadly about what we do," Chalfant says. "But I don't really want to create more competition for myself."

"Come on, John," I insist. "Your success is an inspiration for every dealer and used vehicle manager at a very tough time in our business. What's your secret?"

"Dale, I can't do it."

"Now I know why you thought you'd make a good lawyer," I say. He laughs.

"Let's just say we've done away with the 'golden gut,'" offers Chalfant, who had considered becoming a lawyer before joining the family business. "We make our decisions—purchasing, pricing, and wholesaling—based on data, not instinct. We have taken the emotion out of the deal. That's the moral of our story."

Ahhhh. Now we're getting somewhere, I think.

I ask a softer question: "How is it that you wound up managing the used vehicle department?"

"My uncle, my dad, and our GM thought I'd be good at it," Chalfant says. "We'd been having trouble dealing with the wild fluctuations in used car prices. We were taking massive wholesale hits. We were having a hard time acquiring product at local auctions, and we didn't have trade-ins to back us up because new sales volumes had dropped dramatically."

"That's a familiar story these days," I say. "So, the crimp on inventory was causing trouble. What did you do to address that?"

"We thought we had a problem acquiring vehicles," he says. "But when I started, I spent two weeks looking at Manheim and other auctions online and thought, good gracious. There are thousands of vehicles out there every day. Our problem was that we'd only been buying at our local auction where 50 dealers are picking over 300 vehicles. That's just not a broad enough selection."

Chalfant describes the three computer screens on his desk. One shows his inventory and market metrics, which he uses for pricing and setting appraisal and wholesale values. Another serves as his window on wholesale auction run lists and other data across a five-state region. The third screen checks email and monitors live auction feeds. "At any time, I've got 120 vehicles in transit," he says. "Over the last three months I have only bought cars online."

We chat more about his velocity-based used management philosophy and how it has changed the store's operations and the traditional role of used car manager. John spends most of his time doing what can only be described as "inventory engineering," and overseeing the online merchandising of the store's inventory.

It's quickly apparent that Chalfant thinks and works differently than many dealers and used vehicle managers. For example:

> *Take gross profits.* Chalfant doesn't obsess over gross profits on every deal. In fact, he thinks it's an irrelevant metric for determining whether a used vehicle department is humming or not. "I refuse to have a conversation about gross profit per unit (GPU) or per vehicle retail (PVR). I think it neglects the whole story of revenue generation of a car deal," he says. Instead, he focuses on a new breed of metrics—Cost to Market, Price to Market, and Market Days Supply—to guide his inventory decisions.

Take Gross Profits

Chalfant doesn't obsess over gross profits on every deal. In fact, he thinks it's an irrelevant metric for determining whether a used vehicle department is humming or not. "I refuse to have a conversation about gross profit per unit (GPU) or per vehicle retail (PVR). I think it neglects the whole story of revenue generation of a car deal," he says.

Take his inventory engineering. Chalfant isn't managing inventory age; he's managing the seven-figure investment his inventory represents. In practical terms, this means age is a secondary factor. Chalfant makes pricing changes much more frequently than traditional dealers and used vehicle managers. He bases these pricing changes on market metrics, not educated guesswork. He'll also dispose of a vehicle much faster than other stores—irrespective of its time in inventory—if the metrics indicate it'll be a drag on ROI.

Take his view of today's customers. "They are more educated," he says. "They understand what's out there and what it's going for." As a result, Chalfant views sales as a process where transparency, shared knowledge, and limited negotiation are the new orders of the day. He doesn't resent the fact that his customers are better armed; he embraces it.

Take his reconditioning process. Here, Chalfant definitely doesn't want to go into "huge detail" about the system he's built to ensure efficient throughputs of vehicles for reconditioning. He knows this is a make-or-break aspect of a velocity-based management process. "The service department knows what vehicles have been bought and when they're arriving," he explains. "They're ready for them. I'm pretty popular over there."

Take his online presence. Chalfant knows today's online ROI flows from monitoring metrics like "detailed page views" and conversions to identify potential turnoffs for online customers: inconsistent prices, poor/ missing photos, and dull vehicle descriptions. He's an articulate student of this pixel data, unlike other dealers and used vehicle managers who offer blank stares when I ask about their own online metrics.

As we close our conversation, I'm amazed.

As Chalfant so aptly puts it, good instincts, guesswork, and an unflinching reliance on familiar processes won't cut it anymore. Success today requires better use of data, technology, tools, computer skills, and a conviction to achieve it.

At 25 years old and with only three years of experience in our business, Chalfant impresses me as more knowledgeable about how to guide a used vehicle operation toward success in today's more challenging market than many more seasoned dealers and used vehicle managers—guys who continue to struggle with the same problems he tackled in a short five months. I begin to wonder if his inexperience is actually an asset, given our industry's reluctance to change.

As I think about what Chalfant has accomplished, I realize that his story is one of the more profound examples of the kinds of performance improvement in used vehicles that I'm seeing with increasing frequency as I travel the country to discuss today's business and the challenges it poses. It is fair to say the people who are driving these success stories are either guys like Chalfant, who don't have to undo years of traditional used vehicle management experience to embrace a new way forward, or they're more seasoned dealers and used vehicle managers who, out of necessity or sheer will, have the courage to change processes they've relied on for years.

Chalfant's story also foreshadows the problems that will inevitably develop as dealers and used vehicle managers recognize that what they don't know about today's more challenging used vehicle marketplace is hurting them, and what they do know isn't helping very much.

The conflicts include the inevitable clash when technology-driven efficiencies meet people-driven inefficiencies, and the struggle between change agents and those who, either by fear, disbelief, or lack of skill/interest, resist change.

Chalfant is a shining example of someone whose success highlights what occurs when dealerships adopt the new thinking and processes necessary to drive improved profitability.

I congratulate Chalfant on his success and appreciate his willingness to share that success—if not his secret—to help other dealers chart their own course for success in a more challenging used vehicle marketplace.

A Look Back at "The Old Ways"

Across the country, dealers and used vehicle managers are facing the kind of wholesale losses and diminished sales problems that John Chalfant tidied up in a hurry.

These problems appear to be indiscriminate. They are happening at stores that our industry has long regarded as top-shelf success stories, at dealer groups in metro markets as well as at single-point stores in small towns. What's worse, they are happening despite the best efforts of dealers and used vehicle managers to address them.

Dealer Clay Close of Atchison (Kansas) Automotive knows this frustrating scenario all too well. He bought his four-point GM store in 2007 and gave his "I'm the new boss" speech on the day the Dow Jones average hit 14,000 and national unemployment was about 4 percent.

"It was downhill from there," says Close, a 30-year auto retailing veteran.

In late 2008, he carried an 80-unit inventory in a truck- and SUV-friendly market, and saw wholesale losses and reduced floor traffic that almost put him out of business. "There was nobody coming in here to lay down for $3,000 on a car," Close says. "I realized that I was either going to have to start sending out applications to work for someone else or do something different."

The something different came with Close's decision to adopt the velocity-based principles that Chalfant successfully utilizes. He's trimmed his inventory to about 50 vehicles and focuses on turning them quickly to avoid the risk of costly drops in market values. He uses live market-based tools to set online pricing that attracts buyers from a wider geographic range than he'd previously targeted. He's making rather than losing money, averaging about 50 used deals a month.

"I can live forever doing this," he says. "Once we get out of the recession, we'll start looking at building this up and making some real do-re-mi."

Close's turnaround highlights the underlying dilemma for dealerships today: Our industry is struggling to adapt to a used vehicle marketplace that's faster and more risk-prone than it has ever been. Meanwhile, the prevailing "what to do wisdom" hasn't kept up with the market's pace of change. Sure, we've got "45 is the new 60," vehicle "sets," and other changes on the traditional used vehicle management theme.

But I view these as signs of "tradition" under strain rather than a solution to achieve sustainable success. A fast-moving market requires fast-moving management metrics, tools, and techniques—the fundamental elements of the velocity-based approach that Close and Chalfant use to succeed.

It's no wonder many dealers and used vehicle managers complain that while they're putting more time and attention into their used vehicle operations, they are not gaining any ground.

I'm in a unique position to observe this historical convergence between our industry's traditional used vehicle management practices and the new marketplace. I was a student/disciple of the traditional management practices at our Cadillac store in Elmhurst, Ill., in the mid-1980s. I understand how they work, and recognize their obvious appeal: They're familiar and they made us good money for a very, very long time.

I've since taken what I learned from my time as a dealer and built a company, vAuto, Inc. Our whole purpose is to help dealers and managers understand and capitalize on today's Internet-driven used vehicle market.

So I think there's value in a short trip down memory lane to examine our industry's best practices and why they are less effective than they used to be.

A Confession: What Elmer and I Missed

Elmer was the quintessential used car guy. He'd worked for years in the business and he'd gained a special understanding of the Cadillac brand. He was my right-hand man as the two of us managed used vehicle operations at my family's Cadillac store.

As I think back, there were two underlying beliefs that Elmer and I applied to our used vehicle operations—beliefs that many dealers and used vehicle managers still cling to today:

1. There's an "ass for every seat," and it's just a matter of time before we find the right one for a vehicle.

2. We should always price our vehicles based
    on what we paid for them, whether a unit
    came through a trade-in or at auction.

Taken together, these beliefs touched every aspect of
how we managed the used vehicle department.

Perhaps the most telling example of how these
beliefs affected our management decisions arrived
every week, when our controller, Mike Chiovari,
showed up in our used vehicle office with the general ledger. Mike Chiovari was there at my request.
Our weekly meeting was to review how much negative equity or water we had in our inventory.

The three of us would sit together and dutifully go
through each vehicle, comparing what we'd paid
for the unit and its wholesale value.

The problem? At least 50 percent of the time, Elmer
and I could not agree on what a vehicle was worth
at wholesale. Inevitably, I'd defer to Elmer because
he was our in-house expert who'd spent time at
auctions and knew what a vehicle would bring.

Because Elmer and I often couldn't agree, we rarely
made decisions about getting rid of any inventory
before our 90-day clock had expired. It was only at
or near that time when we'd tweak our pricing and
try to retail out of a vehicle. If a unit hit 90 days
in our inventory it went to auction because I was a

stickler about adhering to our inventory age/turn policy.

In hindsight, I realize that while Elmer and I were following industry best practices for managing our used vehicle operations, our efforts were largely empty gestures.

Our weekly standoff on used vehicle values, and our inability to make a decision to dispose of a vehicle that might pose a problem, meant that Elmer had more time to retail it and earn a hefty gross profit. It's only now that I recognize that Elmer got the better end of the deal—his pay plan emphasized gross profit per vehicle and the more opportunities he had to achieve a hefty gross, the better off he'd be.

From a store perspective, however, I wonder how much better we'd have done if we had dumped those vehicles that appeared questionable during our weekly exercise and found a new unit that might not have been as problematic. Back then, I wasn't aware of what's called an "opportunity cost," or the "benefits you could have received by taking an alternative action.[1]"

But even if I had known or understood the concept of opportunity cost, I'm not sure it would have made a big difference. Both Elmer and I were emo-

---

[1] Forbes' Investopedia, http://www.investopedia.com/terms/o/opportunitycost.asp.

tionally tied to each vehicle and to our own belief
that we'd find an ass for every seat and retail our
way out of what might be a problem.

I have come to understand that there was a second
problem with our weekly exercise and our standoff
on wholesale values. I believe we were focused on
the wrong number. Instead of trying to determine
how much water a vehicle held, we should have
been evaluating its likelihood to sell in order to
meet an investment return objective. In essence, our
weekly exercise should have been spent trying to
get the firmest read possible on whether our "ass
for every seat" belief would prove true and how tall
our vehicle stood in the marketplace.

That's the crux of a velocity-based approach to
used vehicle management. It's based on what I
could never figure out when I was a dealer.

Of course, back in the mid-'80s, the necessary market-based information that's available today didn't
exist. The closest barometer I had was Elmer's
head. He was the guy who knew the market. I now
recognize that I had no empirical way of knowing if
his instincts were correct or not.

A Forgiving Business
Forgives No More

Ah, the good old days. We were happy, flush with hefty profits and the customers kept coming. Today's dealers and used vehicle managers don't have it so easy.

Today's customers know as much, if not more, about specific vehicle values as Elmer and I did when we ran our department. The one-sided nature of our deal-making, which gave us as dealers a distinct advantage, is long gone.

At the same time, Elmer and I faced less competition. For the most part, competition came just from other Cadillac dealers. Dealers with other franchises stuck close to their own brands, as we did ours, when it came to buying and selling used vehicles. In turn, that meant the competitive playing field was smaller. We didn't have to face the encroachment from independents, other franchise dealers, or velocity-minded stores that put additional pressure on most markets today.

Elmer and I had another advantage: We were Cadillac dealers and our customers were largely loyal to the brand. In addition, the "aspirational" aspects of the Cadillac brand meant that our used inventory appealed to buyers who wanted to "step up" to the luxury tier. It was a segment leader that had cache across all household income levels.

Today, the landscape is completely different. Brand loyalties aren't what they used to be. To make the situation worse, today's customers have easy access to websites where they can compare vehicles in any segment against others with similar price points and equipment configurations. Similarly, these websites also allow comparisons between dealers. The idea that any given used vehicle is one of a kind and unique isn't as true as it used to be when you account for how easy it is for customers today to find alternatives.

I'd like to believe that if Elmer and I were still running our used vehicle department, we'd be successful. But there's no way we could keep up with guys like John Chalfant or Clay Close, who use all of today's market data and tools to determine how to acquire, price, merchandise, wholesale, and retail their inventories.

Thankfully, Elmer and I operated in a marketplace that masked and forgave our mistakes. Buyers had little knowledge about whether we were trying to sell at a price that was out of line for the market. And, if they had a clue, we'd use our negotiation skills and Elmer's charm to make them feel good about paying it.

As I listen to the struggles many dealers and used vehicle managers are having today, I'm struck by the degree to which many still follow the same beliefs and operational practices that Elmer and I used over 20 years ago.

But I understand why they remain. It's difficult for anyone to change from something that has worked successfully for so long.

Perhaps the first step toward making this change to a more market-attuned, velocity-based approach to managing used vehicle operations is to understand exactly the kind of market forces we are all up against.

THE GREAT EQUALIZER
ARRIVES—AND THRIVES

It's 10 a.m. in Peoria, Illinois and dealer Bill Pearson's running late.

It's not his fault.

Mechanical difficulties had grounded his flight home the night before, forcing an overnight stay in Chicago. He was back on track this morning, driving from a nearby airport to meet me at his store, Finish Line Ford.

No matter. The delay offers a chance to get a feel for his operation. It's got buzz ... more so than many other Ford stores these days. Salespeople here actually have customers with them—at their desks, on the phone, on the lot and, on their computer screens via the Internet.

The showroom has an air of purpose, a crispness of pace. I hear the sound of a belly laugh from a nearby office, a sign of levity, if not job satisfaction. It's readily apparent, when Pearson arrives, flashes a smile, and apologizes for the lag, where the vibe at Finish Line comes from.

"I'm a sunshine type of person," he says. "It's easy to work for me if you do your job well."

Judging from the results Pearson's achieved in the past two years, he and his entire team are doing their jobs well. He's taken a store that did about 50 used vehicles a month and turned it into a 300-unit-per-month machine. On average, most used vehicles get sold before they hit the 25-day mark in his inventory. He's turning his inventory of 400 vehicles roughly 15 times a year.

I've come to visit Pearson and tour his store to get an insider's view of his operation. Right off the bat, it's apparent that he and the store are attuned to the Internet and velocity-based used vehicle management processes. In fact, they've harnessed both to create a double-barreled, net-profit generating powerhouse.

"I really believe we're an Internet store," Pearson says. "Some dealers think it's not fair that the customer has the Internet and often shops there first. We take the opposite view and go the other way."

I find his statement to be both powerful and painfully true for our industry. There's no question that the Internet has changed our business, and it is dealers like Pearson and John Chalfant who are proving that embracing the Internet's role in the used car-buying process is a key ingredient for a dealership's success. All too often, though, dealers and used vehicle managers bemoan or resent the fact that the Internet is now forcing them to run their stores in a more transparent, customer-friendly and price-conscious manner.

WHY THE INTERNET IS SO POWERFUL AND DISRUPTIVE

It's pretty amazing to think, in 2009, that a 10-year-old company, *Google*, and a roughly 15-year-old phenomenon, the Internet, have become such powerful forces in a business that, for the most part, hasn't changed much in nearly 100 years.

"The Internet is the same everywhere," says Pearson. For him, this means his competition is not the dealer down

The reason the Internet has become such a transformative force in our business is because it has leveled the playing fields between dealers and consumers. It has also opened the door to a wealth of new opportunity.

the street. He sets his mark on other online used vehicle retailers such as Texas Direct, Missouri City, Tex. He estimates nearly half of the 300 units he sells a month go to customers outside of a 75-mile circle from his dealership.

I like to say the Internet has dealt dealers and managers two hands:

> **The bad hand:** This is the one that forces dealers and managers to adopt new ways of pricing and presenting their vehicles that they've not had to consider before. It's the same hand that means a re-set in your sales processes to acknowledge the fact that today's online customers may often know more about an individual vehicle, and comparable alternatives at other stores, than your salespeople.

> **The good hand:** This is the hand Pearson has chosen to play. The Internet provides a steady stream of customers who gather on websites like *AutoTrader.com, Cars.com,* and to some extent, dealers' own websites, looking for vehicles. As Pearson and other dealers have learned, if your price, vehicle, and process are "right" for these customers, getting them to buy is almost a foregone conclusion.

"We don't get people looking to shop for cars online," Pearson says. "They are online to buy a particular car." And when they get to the store, "there's very little or no negotiation. We've already shown them our value online."

This is a striking change for retailing veterans like Clay Close at Atchison Automotive. He came up in the business as a gifted "closer." Now, much of the "closing" happens online. "I sold a guy a Yukon XL the other day. He didn't want a phone call. He wanted to handle the deal while he was at work through email and be done with it. This story happens over and over," Close says.

Given these dynamics, demonstrating online value for today's Internet consumers is absolutely critical to gaining their attention. The Internet is the gateway that determines whether a customer will choose to contact your store or just show up to inquire about a used vehicle.

To make matters more challenging, all this shopping occurs without you knowing it, aside from after-the-fact indicator metrics like detailed page views and search results placements (assuming one knows what those mean and pays attention to them). In this environment, transparency is the order of the day, as is a customer-focused transaction process.

"A lot of dealers think if they're on the Internet, they're in the game," says Chip Perry at *AutoTrader.com*. "That's simply not true."

So what are the factors that drive interest in your store and put new pressures on traditional used vehicle management practices?

Here's a broad, quick look at three critical factors that address why the Internet has been a disruptive force for many traditional dealerships. We'll address these and other factors in more detail in the upcoming chapters:

> **Factor 1–Your Vehicles:** Just as it's always been, the "right" vehicle will find a customer. But there are two key differences in today's Internet-driven marketplace that make stocking the correct inventory a more challenging arena for dealers and used vehicle managers.

First, what you've long considered "right" for your store is not always "right" for your market. When Elmer and I ran our family's used vehicle department, roughly 80 percent of our vehicles were Cadillacs. We believed customers would intuitively shop us for used Cadillacs given the strong appeal of our franchise brand.

While that's still true, it's far less of a motivator for today's buyers. Their loyalties to specific brands have eroded, while their loyalties to finding a vehicle that fits their budget and lifestyle have cemented.

In response, dealers like Pearson are using live market data to show them what vehicles may be "right" for their stores and potential customers—and have the best shot at selling quickly.

At Finish Line, Pearson studied market data that showed untapped demand for luxury vehicles, including Mercedes-Benz, Lexus, and even Lamborghini. "We're supplying pent-up demand in Peoria," he says. "In the past, these buyers would have looked to Chicago or other areas to find these vehicles."

> *"I never dreamed I'd sell a $30,000 Corvette," says dealer Jon Whitman of Whitman Ford, Temperance, Michigan. "But I did the other day. The data told me it would sell and I was brave enough to believe it."*

Make no mistake, Pearson still sells plenty of Fords amongst the 300 sales he achieves every month; but his understanding of consumer interests led him to a segment he likely would not have considered in the past.

Based on the data I see from reviewing live market metrics, I can confidently suggest that today's Internet-enabled marketplace requires a roughly 50/50 mix of franchise to off-brand vehicles in your used vehicle inventory to gain maximum attention and traction with today's less brand-loyal customers.

If you're still in doubt about the need for a more varied mix of inventory, here's a question: Which vehicle brand today has a lock on the used car market?

The answer is none really does. There are definitely some vehicles that are hotter than the next, but no single brand commands every market corner and vehicle segment. Yet, many dealers and used vehicle managers continue to stock their used vehicle inventories as if their franchise brands actually *do* own the market.

Years ago, this made sense. But today it doesn't— not with access to market data to guide inventory stocking decisions. Think about new vehicles, for a moment. Every dealer would jump at the chance to sell as many new Toyota Prius or BMW 3 series units that they could get their hands on. But only dealers with the Toyota and BMW franchises have this opportunity and blessing. Every other dealer is locked out of the action. Except on *used* Toyotas and BMWs. There's nothing stopping any dealer or used vehicle manager from stocking these brands, or any other brand, that the market deems a hot seller.

I believe it is far better for dealerships to position their used vehicle inventories to maximize their ability to attract all customers, irrespective of brand. The key is paying attention to the available market data and adjusting used vehicle inventories to reflect market demand for specific makes and models.

That's been an eye-opening change for dealers like Pearson and Whitman. Because they had the courage to make this shift, they are now enjoying the benefits of additional sales volumes and profits at the expense of their more franchise-focused competitors.

You do not have to be the lowest-priced dealer on every unit to attract customers and achieve your profit expectations.

Factor 2–Your Pricing: Before we discuss online pricing dynamics, I need to clear up a misconception that I still hear among dealers and used vehicle managers—a perspective that owes more to yesterday's philosophy for setting used vehicle prices than the realities of today's buyers.

You do not have to be the lowest-priced dealer on every unit to attract customers and achieve your profit expectations.

There it is. I've said it. For dealers and used vehicle managers who believe the Internet is simply a game of low-price leaders and too-low gross profits, I must implore you to "take the road to Damascus and have a Saul-like moment." [2]

The idea that the Internet is solely a place for low-price vehicles misses the fact that *all buyers* use the Web to shop. These buyers care about price, and there is a correlation between the price you set and the attention you'll get from online buyers.

---

[2] *The Holy Bible,* "The Book of Acts," Chapter 9, v. 3-9

But these dynamics do not mean a race to the bottom to find the lowest-price vehicles. The key in an Internet-driven marketplace is to make sure your pricing is competitive and, if it's above market averages, to ensure your vehicles tell a story that merits your asking price.

One of the key problems here is that many dealers and used vehicle managers still use the "mark up from cost" approach to pricing their used vehicle inventory that Elmer and I followed at my family's Cadillac store.

In today's marketplace, this is a pricing strategy that's problematic. Let's examine why.

First, when consumers search for vehicles, they're typically using a third-party site like *AutoTrader.com* or *Cars.com* to view a broad selection of units and prices. Each of these platforms allows customers to sort from lowest to highest to create a price pecking order.

Guess what this means if your vehicle has the highest price as a result of your reflexive, mark-up-from-cost approach to pricing? I can't emphatically predict you'll be out of the running as the consumer shops and selects, but it's fair to say you'll get far less attention than that vehicle may well deserve.

Second, and perhaps most important, is the fact that a mark-up-from-cost pricing approach is based on a faulty presumption that how much you paid for a vehicle has any bearing on what a customer should pay. The fact is, consumers don't care, nor should they, how much you paid for a vehicle. What they care about is how much it will cost them to own it.

"What you paid for a vehicle is important, but with the Internet, it's more important to know potential selling price and the vehicle's likelihood to sell at that price," Pearson says. "From there, you can figure out what kind of gross profit and time in inventory you can expect."

I recognize this is a 180-degree shift in thinking for many dealers and used vehicle managers. So let's drill into why our industry's traditional mark-up-from-cost approach is a problem for today's Internet-driven marketplace.

For example, in the summer of 2009, the wholesale marketplace was on fire. More dealers than ever were in the used vehicle game and the collective demand was pushing up wholesale values.

Let's say a used vehicle manager acquired a three-year-old Honda Accord for $10,000 at auction. The price, the manager knows, is inflated because he and other buyers were bidding strong to own it. (I call this type of "irrational exuberance"[3] a herd mentality—a dangerous auction dynamic.)

---

[3] *Irrational Exuberance*, Robert Shiller,

The manager brings the vehicle to the store and adds a $3,500 mark-up to set a $13,500 asking price. The goal here is a gross profit of $3,500 if the store can get it, or something around $2,000 after negotiation.

So far, so good—except that all the other similar model year Honda Accords are listed in this used vehicle manager's marketplace for $11,500.

In this scenario, the Accord at $13,500 probably won't get much online attention because it's priced at 117 percent of market—in other words, it is listed at a 17% premium to the average price of identically equipped vehicles in the market. What's more, the store's used vehicle manager probably knew he'd paid too much at auction, but had no choice: The store needs inventory to keep sales moving.

The problem, however, is that the $3,500 mark-up from cost means the store is effectively asking a potential buyer to cover the cost of an acquisition mistake. (In the old days, that might have worked, but today's customers know a whole lot more about the going rate for vehicles.) I would suggest that this vehicle is destined to become a problem and, potentially, a wholesale loss for this store.

Now, let's flip the exercise. Say the used vehicle manager got really lucky and stole a three-year-

old Honda Accord on a trade-in for $7,500.
What are the chances the manager would add a
$3,500 mark-up-from-cost and price the vehicle at
$11,000?

Pretty minimal, I would suggest.

Instead, I'll bet the manager would have an instinc-
tive feel that an asking price of $11,000 is better
than the market and set an asking price of $12,500.
Why? Because the manager is aiming for a hefty
"four-pounder" gross profit and expecting it might
end up around $3,000. Here again, a perfectly
good vehicle may end up becoming an aged unit
because the mark-up did not reflect the market's
average asking price.

By contrast, here's what I believe velocity-minded
dealers like Pearson, Close, and Chalfant would
do: They'd take the vehicle they "stole," and set
an asking price at or near the $11,500 average for
similar Accords. They might even beat the market
average because they're in the vehicle so "right" to
begin with.

Either way, I'd bet these dealers would sell the unit
much faster than the used vehicle manager who
set a too-high asking price and they'd then be
able to put another used Accord in their inventory
and repeat the cycle. At Pearson's store, where the
average days in inventory runs about 25 days, he'd
likely sell two used Accords while the traditional

used vehicle manager is still trying to sell the one
unit he acquired for a song.

Now, don't get me wrong. I'm not suggesting dealers and used vehicle managers should not exercise
their right to achieve maximum gross profits. I'm
simply trying to point out that the "old school way"
of marking up vehicles from cost carries a greater
risk for your store than a more market-attuned
approach to pricing.

As Pearson says, "you've got to pick your spots to
play."

> **Factor 3–Your Presentation:** I noted above
> that much of the online action for used vehicle
> buyers occurs on third-party listing sites like
> *AutoTrader.com* and *Cars.com*.

So, if a consumer searches for a 2007 Honda
Accord, each site will list those units from dealers
who've got them. We've noted how, if a dealer's
asking price is out of line with market expectations,
consumers will likely scroll right past a listing,
unless a dealer or used vehicle manager makes it
abundantly clear why the vehicle should command
bigger dollars.

Similarly, the dealers and used vehicle managers
who offer '07 Accords at competitive prices also
must make sure that their presentation of this
vehicle online—from photos to detailed descrip-

tions—offers a compelling reason for an online shopper to take a closer look.

The key: The challenge for today's used vehicle retailers becomes how to present vehicles online in a manner that distinguishes and differentiates them from competitors when these units appear as one of many on a shopper's computer screen.

"Dealers have their physical showroom and their virtual showroom," says Perry at *AutoTrader.com*. "Pictures and vehicle descriptions are critically important. We still see dealers taking shortcuts."

Pearson goes a step further. "You can't miss on anything—whether it's price, pictures, mileage, video, equipment," he says. "I pay extremely close attention to how our vehicles look online. We're always trying to improve our online presentation."

Pearson and other velocity dealers recognize that effective online presentation and merchandising of vehicles requires a great deal of time and special skills. Each of them has tapped support from others at their store to get the job done right.

At many stores, however, the used vehicle manager ends up with the responsibility for handling the online presentation—on top of other responsibilities like managing inventory, taking TOs, and desking deals. I would submit that this amounts to an overload of responsibility on one person, making everything this individual does less effective overall.

"Everyone's pressed for time," says *Cars.com* president Mitch Golub, who acknowledges compelling presentation is essential for online used vehicle retailing success. "The question is how to reinvent how the work gets allocated and investing the time and energy into doing it right."

TWO KEY INTERNET BLESSINGS

If nothing else, I hope this chapter's review of the Internet's role in used vehicle retailing success gets dealers and managers thinking hard about how they should adjust their inventory management, pricing, and merchandising approaches to better fit the expectations and needs of today's consumers.

Before we move into discussing another disruptive factor for today's dealers and used vehicle managers in the next chapter, I'd like to share a little more on the "good hand" the Internet has dealt our industry.

I mentioned above that the Internet makes it much more cost-effective and easy for dealers and used vehicle managers to connect with customers. They are, after all, using the Internet to find and make choices for the used vehicles they intend to purchase.

Beyond that, however, the Internet has also provided a window that makes possible the kind of velocity-based management metrics that dealers like Pearson, Chalfant, and Close use.

For example, my company, vAuto, Inc., uses proprietary technology to search the Internet for data on vehicle sales rates, retail asking prices, and other data that help dealers manage their online presentation and inventory decisions more effectively. This is competitive market intelligence that would not exist without the Internet.

Likewise, activity on the Internet is infinitely measurable. That means dealers who use vendors like *AutoTrader.com* and *Cars.com* have ready access to metrics that detail their online merchandising effectiveness. I've added another layer to these metrics, using the experiences of vAuto's clients to develop benchmarks for what success means in terms of the amount of time and attention consumers give to an individual dealer's online inventory.

For a dealer like Pearson, the blessings the Internet offers in terms of access to customers and measurable results, plus his adoption of velocity-based used vehicle management practices, have given him a renewed lease on his auto retailing career.

"I was truly debating getting out of the business," says Pearson, who had purchased Finish Line with respected Peoria dealer Jeff Green in 2006. For two years, he struggled. "It was brain damage," he says. "We weren't having any fun and we weren't making any money."

Now, Pearson has a different management dilemma: how to feed and manage what has become a net-profit generating machine. For him, it means weekly trips traversing the country to source vehicles to maintain his inventory supply and turn rates.

"The question is how far we can take this?" he says. "It definitely takes intestinal fortitude to jump in."

HELLO,
MR. EFFICIENT MARKET

In the fall of 2008, like many dealers, Dan Sunderland realized he had a problem with used vehicles.

He had opened a new Mercedes-Benz store the past June for his four-franchise dealership Sun Motor Cars in Mechanicsburg, Pa. By autumn, following big spikes in gas prices and the grip of a recession, Sunderland and his used vehicle manager, Steve Barnes, realized they were losing ground.

"We were having trouble turning our cars," Sunderland says. "We began to have problems with aging
vehicles and wholesale losses."

Barnes estimates the store's inventory water neared
$200,000 with gross profits on the units they sold
only averaging about $2,400—much less than the
$3,500 PVR they'd been accustomed to in prior
years.

A few states west, dealer Keith Kocourek faced
similar problems at his Wausau, Wis. store. "Sep-
tember 2008 through December 2008 were the
worst four sales months we've had in our history,"
Kocourek says. "Our wholesale losses were north
of $200,000." As he evaluated his inventory, he
found nearly half of his vehicles were older than 60
days—a symptom of holding out for buyers who
just were there.

Germain Motor Company in Columbus, Ohio tells
a similar story. Six-figure wholesale losses combined with slowing sales spurred the dealer group
to look for a new process to help address their
persistent used vehicle problems, according to John
Malishenko, director of operations for the nine-
store dealer group.

"There was an urgent need to change the way we
were doing things," Malishenko says. "What we
had done historically wasn't working anymore.

"We had a static strategy in an erratic marketplace," he explains. "With a velocity mindset, we now have a dynamic strategy that changes with the market—whether it's the vehicles we buy, the reconditioning we do, or the prices we set."

Wow. Thank you, John! He hit the nail on the head.

I believe that a velocity-based approach to managing used vehicles offers a solution that, as Malishenko says, moves with market conditions. If the market goes suddenly south, dealers and used vehicle managers who follow velocity metrics and principles will inevitably see the signs of trouble sooner and be able to respond more quickly than those who continue to rely on traditional management best practices.

"It's working for us," says Malishenko, who notes wholesale losses have been cut by $340,000 and volumes are surpassing store records set in 2007. "In the middle of a recession and the worst economy in years, we're selling a record number of used vehicles."

The reason used vehicle management troubles persist is because there are dealers that continue to operate with a match-up that doesn't work. They are fighting a volatile market without the philosophy, technology, and processes that enable them to respond to rapid change. It's like "rope-a-dope" with an opponent who never tires.[1] No wonder dealers and used vehicle managers are frustrated by a lack of results.

---

[1] Muhammad Ali, http://en.wikipedia.org/wiki/Rope-a-dope

I also believe that the volatile market conditions that emerged in 2008 and 2009 are the final signs of a transformation of the used vehicle marketplace from one that's traditionally been highly inefficient to one that grows more efficient with each passing day. The Internet plays a starring role in this transformation, with supporting roles going to the sagging economy, gas price swings, factory closures, and lender belt-tightening.

AN EFFICIENT MARKET MEETS INEFFICIENT PROCESSES

Economists describe a market as "efficient" when there is roughly equal knowledge between buyers and sellers of choices and alternatives and, as a result, the prices are governed largely by supply, demand, and price sensitivity.

Let's break this down a bit.

> *Is there equal knowledge between buyers and sellers in today's used vehicle marketplace?*
> In the last chapter, we discussed how the Internet is the "great equalizer" that arms consumers with more information about vehicle prices, equipment/trim levels, owner histories, wholesale values, and dealers' reputations than they've ever had before. It's not uncommon for customers to bring printouts of competing vehicles when they come to stores—just to let

dealers and used vehicle managers know they've got a bead on the market. So, to answer the question, while the knowledge may not be 100 percent equal, it's enough to alter the dynamics of traditional deal-making. Likewise, whatever knowledge gap may exist is shrinking on a daily basis.

Are used vehicles commodities? I get this question a lot when I talk about efficient markets with dealers and used vehicle managers. In their view, it's impossible for a vehicle to be a commodity since "every vehicle is unique." My view is more nuanced: Every vehicle definitely has an individual value story. But there's little that's unique about an '07 Honda Accord when a consumer can readily find dozens of comparable vehicles with similar colors and equipment/trim packages at the click of a mouse. In this sense, used vehicles are commodities, and I believe they should be managed and retailed with the same mindset as those who work in a commodities market—that is, with a key understanding of market data and dynamics so as to effectively and efficiently mitigate risks to investment returns.

Is the price of today's used vehicles determined by supply, demand, and price sensitivity? The answer to this question, in my view, is an unequivocal "yes." What happened to dealers

Sunderland, Kocourek, and Malishenko in late 2008? Their problems in used vehicles were a direct result of higher gas prices and less interest among financially troubled consumers to purchase vehicles. In turn, these more circumspect consumers were less likely to buy vehicles that bore traditional mark-ups to achieve gross profit expectations at dealerships. The end result was widespread difficulty at dealerships with aging vehicles and wholesale losses.

"We'd spend $1,500 on a car to recondition it, put it on the lot and price it to make $4,000," Malishenko says. "We'd sit there and wait for someone to come in. The car would get 90 days old and, because we'd spent money on reconditioning and knew we'd get killed at the auction block, we kept it another 30 days."

This traditional approach to managing used vehicles is out of step with today's efficient market. By definition, "waiting for a buyer" is an inefficient way to retail a vehicle. It's a far more dangerous and speculative bet than using a velocity-based approach that ties acquisition, pricing, retailing, and wholesaling decisions to real market data.

"We run our department now based on a calculation of where each vehicle stands in our market," Kocourek says. "It's just logic. There's no guesses, hope, or wishful thinking."

As a result of this more efficient velocity-based approach, Malishenko and his team have achieved their own efficiencies: They invest $6 million less in inventory; turn their vehicles two to three times faster; experience far fewer wholesale losses; and enjoy increasing sales volumes.

"Between the reduction in wholesale losses, the efficiencies of cash we've freed up, our improved sales volumes, and the positive impact on service and F&I, it's a no-brainer," he says.

As I talk with dealers and managers about efficient markets and why I believe today's used vehicle marketplace is increasingly efficient, I note that the concept of an efficient market should not be unfamiliar.

In fact, as I make the case for a velocity-minded approach to managing used vehicle inventories, I'm in many ways suggesting that dealers apply some of the same principles to managing their used inventories as they do with their new vehicle inventories.

On any given day, dealerships follow principles of supply, demand, and price sensitivity when they order new vehicles from factories. To varying degrees, dealers recognize their new vehicles are essentially commodities sold by themselves and competitors.

Dealers base new vehicle ordering decisions on market data from factories and other sources that provide a read on supply and demand projections for sales volumes. It's also true that dealers say "no" to factory reps every day when they get pressure to take additional inventory that, instinctively or empirically, they know will not sell well in their market.

For the most part, these inventory decisions are unemotional. They are calculations based on using the best available data and marketplace dynamics of supply and demand.

Likewise, pricing decisions on new vehicles typically follow market realities. If a new vehicle is "hot," dealers are more likely to sell at or near MSRP, particularly if the supply of these vehicles is scarce. The converse is also true for vehicles with high supply and less demand. These units are far less likely to command MSRP.

Part of the reason for more market-attuned pricing on new vehicles flows from dealers understanding that prospective buyers have equal knowledge about invoice pricing and retail asking prices, as well as incentives. Today's consumers can easily access this data and shop to find the dealership that offers what they believe is the best deal.

It's fair to say that most dealerships at least initially organized their Internet departments and business development centers around prospective new vehicle buyers in recognition of the more efficient nature of this marketplace.

To me, it's ironic that while new vehicle departments operate with an understanding of marketplace efficiencies, this thinking has been largely absent in used vehicle departments. The signs of this dichotomy are readily apparent:

- Used vehicle inventories typically skew toward a franchised brand, rather than account for supply and demand for off-brand vehicles that could prove to be good sellers. In essence, used vehicle managers continue to "go with what they know."

- Pricing decisions reflect what a store paid for a vehicle rather than an assessment of the going market rate for a vehicle.

- Acquisition and wholesale decisions often reflect the biases and emotions of the used vehicle manager who's in charge of making them. Given that it is assumed that a "good used vehicle manager" typically represents someone who "knows" used vehicles, there's deference given to this knowledge, whether it's warranted or not. A decision to "retail out of a problem" owes more to this up-front emotional investment than any firm gauge on whether the market will reward that decision.

When I highlight the contrast in management philosophies between new and used vehicles, many dealers and used vehicle managers start to see why they continue to struggle. They recognize that they're battling an efficient market with inefficient management practices. Some take this realization further, and commit themselves to operating in a way that's more agile and attuned to today's faster-moving and more efficient used vehicle marketplace.

Standstill Speculation Versus ROI-Minded Retailing

For much of the past three years, I've had the privilege of working with one of our country's finest dealer groups, a group that has been an industry innovator, sales leader, and household name for years.

On a recent visit to the group's main store, I sat with the used vehicle manager and other top executives to examine why the store's used vehicle volumes have dropped by about 50 percent and why, after months of effort, they still hadn't been able to move the sales needle.

On the surface, the dynamics at this store are the same as many dealerships across the country—even with the store's enviable West Coast location and reputation: New sales had dropped for the store's domestic franchise brand, sapping trade-ins that

normally fueled the used vehicle department. Likewise, the store had trouble finding vehicles it could
purchase at auction, given an upward swing in
wholesale values due to greater competition among
buyers in the auction lanes.

But a deeper examination revealed other problems
that, when taken together, amounted to a standstill
in their used vehicle department.

- The store still emphasized its franchise brand,
  with 80 percent of its used inventory reflecting
  the nameplate. As we reviewed marketplace
  dynamics, the store had virtually none of the
  off-brand highline models that were selling
  like hotcakes, nor did it stock enough off-
  brand, "plain Jane" units that, while not as
  exciting as sports cars and other snazzy units
  the store preferred to stock, were selling at
  faster rates.

- The store's average days in inventory ran well
  above 100 days. Its retail asking prices were,
  on average, 10 percent above the market if not
  more. Both of these, I learned, were symptom-
  atic of a dealership goal of generating $3,000
  gross profit per unit.

- The store did not show any wholesale losses
  on the books. I was mystified, although a
  deeper discussion revealed that "packs" and
  "moving money around" likely masked the
  true wholesale loss picture.

- The store had not taken any steps to acquire inventory beyond a local auction or two—despite acknowledging that more aggressive sourcing was likely needed.

As I discussed these dynamics, it became clear that the dealership's desire to achieve its gross profit goal on every vehicle was undermining its ability to become a more efficient and market-attuned used vehicle retailer. In addition, the management practices that masked the true costs of their inefficient processes also inhibited the store's ability to transform to a new used vehicle management model.

So while this store stands still, here's what's happening in the fast-moving, more efficient marketplace that surrounds it:

> **Wholesale Value Volatility:** At the time of writing, the wholesale values of used vehicles are increasing, not falling as they had been the previous year. Manheim Consulting says the reversal is the result of a drop-off in new vehicle sales, diminished supplies of used vehicles at auctions, and greater demand for vehicles from wholesale buyers (essentially the dealers and used vehicle managers who've made used vehicles a priority in the past 12 months).[4]

---

[4] Manheim Consulting, http://www.manheimconsulting.com/
Used_Vehicle_Value_Index/Current_Monthly_Index.html

"I used to look at inventory age reports once a month and now I look at them daily," says Steve Barnes at Sun Motor Cars. *"In the past, I didn't re-price some vehicles from the day I bought them until I sold them. Now I evaluate where a car stands in the marketplace and re-price at day 10, day 15 or wherever I need to. This stuff didn't happen before. Now we focus on it daily."*

Lender Volatility: The rise in wholesale vehicle values is contributing to a pincer-like effect on deal-making at dealerships. Lenders, who are retrenching from losses and recalculating risk, are less likely to pay as much advance on deals, and they're far less likely to absorb any negative equity than they did in deals just a few years ago. This dynamic, which I view as another sign of marketplace volatility, means dealers and used vehicle managers must be attuned to the vehicles and customer credit profiles that can and will get the ultimate OK from lenders.

"We have our list of vehicles that we know will give us the best shot with lenders and F&I product penetration," says the GM for a South Carolina store that's adopted velocity management principles. "It's typically fast-moving stuff like '08 Impalas and Ford 500s."

Consumer Volatility: As noted above, today's consumers are more circumspect than in the past about spending money on big purchases like used vehicles. What's more, their interest in buying is more erratic: If gas prices are going up, they move toward fuel-efficient vehicles. If gas prices stabilize, the market for SUVs and trucks picks up.

These market nuances are lost on traditional dealers and used vehicle managers like my West Coast dealer friend who effectively stocks and sells what he knows instead of determining the vehicle segments where demand bubbles are building and breaking.

"With a static strategy in a dynamic market, you might get lucky and find that your strategy meshes with the market," Malishenko says. "More often than not, though, you're missing opportunities."

The key take-away: An efficient market, with its innate volatility, creates risk for dealers and used vehicle managers. The longer a vehicle stays in a store's inventory, the greater the chance that wholesale value changes, shifts in consumer preferences, and other factors will impede a vehicle's ability to sell and produce an acceptable ROI. Likewise, the longer a vehicle remains in inventory, the longer a dealer's investment is tied up in a unit that may be a less effective retailing proposition than another.

Meanwhile, a velocity-based approach to managing used vehicle operations by its "from money to metal, money to metal" nature, reduces risk by enabling dealers and used vehicle managers to efficiently track marketplace dynamics and sell vehicles in a shorter time to minimize exposure to the market's volatility.

"There's no going back to the way we used to do things," says Sunderland at Sun Motor Cars.

AN INTRODUCTION TO
VELOCITY METRICS

As the guy who oversees used vehicle operations at Irwin Motors in Laconia, New Hampshire, Chris Irwin isn't what you might consider a typical used car guy.

He's 25, with only minimal experience in a dealership, much less a used vehicle department. He doesn't go to auctions. He doesn't appraise vehicles. He's not on the front line.

Yet Irwin has managed to achieve results in his used vehicle department that guys twice his age, with 15 times more experience, have not been able to accomplish.

"We've got a first-class problem now," says Irwin, the store's vice president, who also oversees F&I, service, and parts departments. "We're selling our vehicles faster than we can replace them."

Irwin's store is cranking through its inventory. The store sells about 70 units a month out of a 60-vehicle inventory. He's on a trajectory to turn this nearly $800,000 inventory investment 15 times this year, generating an estimated $200,000 return every time it flips. He's freed up cash for the store. He's making his F&I and service teams happy. He has plans to grow his sales volume and inventory investment.

"We've got a first-class problem now," says Irwin, the store's vice president who also oversees F&I, service, and parts departments. "We're selling our vehicles faster than we can replace them."

So goes the power of a live market, velocity-minded approach to managing used vehicle operations. It can help someone like Irwin who, by traditional standards, lacks the experience necessary for success in used vehicles.

The key to his success is his commitment to a velocity-based management philosophy and a near-religious devotion to the market-based metrics that make it hum. These metrics give Irwin the real-time market information he needs to make informed decisions about what to stock, what to pay, how to price, and how to adjust his inventory to meet market conditions.

To be sure, Irwin's not in it alone, nor are the metrics the sole reason for his success. He leads a team of players who possess the traditional paint expertise and the skills to complement his knack for understanding metrics-based data. This group handles the tasks of acquiring, merchandising, and reconditioning vehicles. Collectively, they've created and maintained a velocity-focused process that has the results to prove it's working.

"We had the same mentality that's typical of most stores—we were trying to hit a home run by getting lucky by having somebody stumble into a vehicle on our lot," he says.

With the market turmoil of late 2008 and 2009, Irwin took it on the chin as they retailed their way out of a watered-down inventory. He knew there was a better way. He launched the velocity-based approach to address the persistent issues they encountered with traditional management practices and went after the huge opportunity Irwin believed the store could achieve in used vehicles.

Now, Irwin's team has sourcing and stocking issues—and less concern about any damage caused by fast-moving swings in the market.

"When you take into account market supply and demand, and price yourself aggressively to the market, you're essentially hedging yourself against gasoline and vehicle price fluctuations," he says.

"You're able to react very quickly. You're nimble. You don't get stuck with something that you don't own right and can't get out from under. Even when you have market volatility, you can remain very profitable."

The turnaround success Irwin has achieved is a story that's similar to the experiences of other stores where leaders and managers have adopted a velocity-based approach to managing used vehicle operations.

The foundation for this approach lies in three key paint-oriented metrics that effectively replace, but do not eliminate, the traditional barometers dealers and used vehicle managers have relied on to manage their used vehicle departments. The metrics offer a more reliable gauge for the dynamism and volatility of today's efficient used vehicle marketplace, and they do a better job of helping dealers and used vehicle managers like Irwin mitigate the risks this new marketplace poses for their inventory investments.

Jack Anderson, the director of used vehicle operations for Buffalo, N.Y.-based West Herr Automotive Group credits velocity-based metrics for helping his stores achieve 20 percent growth in used vehicle volumes (about 1,000 units/month) in the past year.

So far in 2009, Anderson's stores have sold more than 400 Dodge Avengers, based on his read of market supply and demand and pricing metrics for the units that showed them as financing-favorable "switch" cars other dealers might overlook. He started with a mass buy of 150 units, and has since kept them rolling through his inventory.

"Other dealers call me to get them," he says. "We're not afraid to take a chance if we know we can absorb the risk."

As dealerships adopt market-attuned metrics, the time-honored measures, such as PVR, a vehicle's average time in inventory, negative equity, 45- or 60-day turn policy performance and the like, remain important. But I would submit the new metrics should take priority[5].

In the next three chapters, we'll discuss these new, velocity-style metrics that address the paint side of our business in great detail—Market Days Supply, Price to Market, and Cost to Market. We'll define how they came about, what they mean, and how they play out in day-to-day used vehicle management decisions for guys like Irwin and others who use them to drive success.

---

[5] A disclosure: I've developed these metrics in tandem with my team at vAuto. So, I have a vested interest. But I believe the success of velocity-focused dealers is a testament to the efficacy of these metrics as operational benchmarks for any dealer or used vehicle manager.

After we've established these new benchmarks for the paint side of used vehicle management, we'll address another set of essential metrics. These metrics give dealers and used vehicle managers the management insights and intelligence they need to be efficient, competitive, and profitable players with their online merchandising, or the "pixel" side of today's business.

"Paint" Metric 1 :
Market Days Supply

Chris Irwin pays close attention to the Market Days Supply of his inventory for a couple of reasons.

It gives him a key read on the vehicles that will sell well in his market. And it works. He's selling vehicles as fast as he can find them.

The Market Days Supply metric will also be Irwin's guide to take his used vehicle operations to the next level.

"We want to crank this up," he says. "We can stock more of the right units that are selling in our market and ultimately sell more of them."

The definition of Market Days Supply is straight-forward. It is the current available supply of a given vehicle in a market divided by the average retail sales rate for the vehicle over the past 45 days.

So, if there were 10 vehicles of the same year, make, model, trim, and identical equipment in a market-place, and they had sold at the retail rate of one per day during the past 45 days, the car would have a market days supply of 10.

The Market Days Supply metric flows from track-ing used vehicle supplies and sales rates across the country and in each market through the use of sophisticated technology. This data-driven market intelligence allows managers to compare the units they might buy or own against the identically equipped, competing vehicles in their market areas.

Market Days Supply

DEFINITION:

Current available market supply

Average daily retail sale rate over the past 45 days

When dealerships know the Market Days Supply when appraising or trading for a '07 Volkswagen Jetta, they will know exactly how many other identical '07 Jettas they will compete against in their market if they acquire the vehicle. The Market Days Supply metric also gives them insight as to how fast they are likely to sell the car.

This is a powerful metric to aid stocking decisions at any dealership. It enables dealership personnel to fine tune their inventory by stocking a greater share of vehicles that have high demand and low supply in their markets—*i.e.*, those units with a low Market Days Supply.

Conversely, it helps them avoid going too heavy with high supply and low demand inventory—*i.e.*, vehicles with a high Market Days Supply.

Market Days Supply provides a window into what used vehicle shoppers want in any given market. It takes the gut and guesswork out of stocking decisions. Dealers and used vehicle managers no longer have to base their inventory decisions on what they *think* will sell or what they are accustomed to selling. The Market Days Supply tells them exactly what is selling in their market.

Understanding and using this metric is a critical first step for dealers who want to adopt a more market-attuned, velocity-based approach to managing their used vehicle operations.

A Look at How Market Days Supply Works

The following composite offers a snapshot view of the Market Days Supply for the used vehicle inventories at three different dealerships in the same market.

The first is a velocity dealer that uses the Market Days Supply to aid in stocking decisions. The two other stores represent traditional dealers, who use prevailing industry best practices to manage their inventories.

The composite tells an interesting tale.

At first glance, which store appears best positioned, before the dealership doors open and the lights go on in the morning, to have a better day? Which store will attract more customers and potentially sell its vehicles more quickly?

The answer should be obvious: The velocity dealer has an average Market Days Supply for its inventory that's less than half that of its closest traditional competitor, regardless of how long those vehicles have been in each dealer's inventory.

This take-away raises several questions. What does the velocity dealer know that the other stores don't? Why does the velocity dealer's inventory possess the winning product characteristics any retailer would

Days in Inventory	Key Metric	Velocity Dealer	Traditional Dealer #1	Traditional Dealer #2
1-30	Market Days Supply	32	67	114
31-60	Market Days Supply	34	73	104
61-90	Market Days Supply	–	76	87

want—high demand and low supply—while the traditional stores seem to have a knack for stocking vehicles that are perhaps more familiar, but that the market is less interested in buying? Why is the concept of a used car Market Days Supply seldom utilized?

Let's address these one at a time:

Question 1: What does the velocity dealer know that the other stores don't?

For starters, he or she knows the Market Days Supply metric exists and uses it.

The metric would not have been possible without the advent and advancement of the Internet and related technology that allows real-time reads of vehicles available in a market, and the aggregation and normalization of sales data down to specific trim and equipment levels and factory certifications on individual vehicles in any market.

The upshot here is that no dealer or used vehicle manager should feel they've been asleep at the switch. This is new stuff. Market Days Supply and other critical "paint" metrics strike me as the guideposts for a better way to go about making used vehicle management decisions than the methods our industry has used for years.

Question 2: Why does the velocity dealer's inventory posses the winning product characteristics any retailer would want—high demand and low supply—while the traditional stores seem to have a knack for stocking vehicles that are perhaps more familiar, but that the market is less interested in buying?

The answer to this question has several facets—all of which largely owe to the way dealers and used vehicle managers have traditionally thought about what used vehicles to stock at their stores.

John Malishenko understands what it's like to see an inventory with Market Days Supply metrics like those of the traditional dealers in the composite. It's a snapshot that isn't much different than how inventories looked at Germain stores before they switched over to a velocity-based approach to management.

"The vehicles we typically bought were, in most cases, the make of our new car franchise," Malishenko says. "That's what we thought we should sell. That's what everybody did."

This skew toward franchise brands is a key reason the Market Days Supply at these traditional stores is out of line. In essence, dealers have long gone with what they know, rather than what has the best shot of selling in a marketplace.

I did a study of used vehicle inventory make-ups at different dealerships across the country. On average, most franchised dealerships stock 70 percent of their used vehicle inventory with units that represent their franchised brand.

Based on what I've seen from studying market dynamics across the country, I suggest the optimal inventory mix should be 50/50 between franchise and off-brand vehicles. There are some exceptions, particularly for select brands with strong factory certified programs.

Now, there are good reasons why decision makers have developed this bias toward stocking franchise brands in used vehicle inventories. It flows from a natural desire to avoid costly mistakes. This risk aversion flows from what I call "gotcha!" moments.

Every dealer and used vehicle manager has at least one "gotcha!" moment. It happens most often with off-brand vehicles. A used vehicle manager or buyer acquires a unit that, for all intents and purposes, should be a winner. Then it tanks. Big time.

The problem? The buyer bought the right make/model but with the wrong trim and/or equipment options—a sunroof, entertainment system, navigation, or another feature that would have made the vehicle more desirable to the marketplace.

These gotcha! moments are completely understandable. They occur when a used vehicle manager or buyer steps outside what's familiar and dabbles in off-brand vehicles.

The immediate consequence of such gotcha! moments is also understandable; the used vehicle manager and buyer don't want to make another costly mistake and, in turn, they shy away from purchasing off-brand vehicles. This mentality contributes to the average franchised dealership's used vehicle inventory skewing 70 to 80 percent toward franchised brands. And it means far too many dealerships are not exploiting opportunities outside their franchised brands.

For dealerships that believe they should stock their used vehicle inventories with their franchise brand more heavily than off-brand vehicles I would offer the following observations that I've gleaned from

studying the dynamics of dealership market areas
across the country:

Observation 1: **Ever walk an independent used
vehicle dealer's lot?** If the operator is successful,
it's likely the inventory includes a wide array
of makes and models, and it isn't likely to lean
too heavily toward any particular brand. This
mix is the independent dealership's best guess
at what's likely to sell. It may not be the right
mix for the market, but there's a fairly strong
chance that the mix is better positioned, given
its variety, to appeal to a wider array of buyers
than a franchised store that sticks mainly to its
franchised brand in used vehicles.

Why this difference between independent and
franchised dealer inventories? It's because the
independent lacks the blessings and the baggage
of a franchised brand. This dealer doesn't have the
opportunity to certify vehicles nor is he beholden to
a trade-in supply that might not reflect the best-
selling vehicles for a market. Likewise, the concepts
of "core inventory" that have sprouted alongside
the franchise brand stocking bias do not burden
these independent dealers.

Observation 2: **Today's buyers are less brand
loyal.** As we've noted earlier, the Internet is a
powerful equalizing force. It allows consumers the opportunity to compare similar used

vehicles as they shop. They may have a preference for a given brand, but the ubiquity and availability of all buying options online works to erode any degree of brand loyalty across most vehicle segments. The consequence of this marketplace reality is that customers don't consider a Ford or Infiniti store as the sole place where they can buy used vehicles that carry those brands. For dealership personnel who cling to this old belief, and stock their inventories accordingly, the outcome is often a Market Days Supply that is higher than it should be.

So what's the good news in all this?

First, managers no longer need to fear the "gotcha!" moments. The technology, tools, and the Market Day Supply are now available to minimize the risks. Dealers and used vehicle managers can now identify the myriad of trim and equipment configurations that can make a difference between a winning vehicle and a loser—no matter the brand. They can make "same-same" comparisons on any vehicle.

Another "good news" item is that the Internet makes it a whole lot easier for dealers and used vehicle managers to find buyers when they model their inventory to market demand. When a store stocks the vehicles that the market craves, and prices and presents them in a way that's competitive and effective, buyers will seek them out.

The "Core Inventory" Myth

Most dealers and used vehicle managers have heard the term "core inventory." By definition, this is the inventory that's ostensibly the "right" inventory for a given store, given its past sales history.

This concept is problematic and has a corrosive effect on a dealership's ability to build sales volume and profits in their used vehicle departments.

Why? For starters, most dealers and used vehicle managers have built their used vehicle departments around selling the makes/models that match their franchise. It's this inventory and past selling history that defines the core products they should sell.

The problem is that the store's franchised brand bias doesn't offer a true picture of what is selling in the dealership's market area. What if it's a Ford store that's historically stocked 80 percent of its lot with Blue Opal models? Would its core inventory reflect the fast-moving pre-owned Camrys that the Toyota dealer up the street is selling?

It's far better for dealers and used vehicle managers to tune their inventories to supply and demand dynamics of the market, not past performance.

Metrics like Market Days Supply can guide such market-based stocking decisions and help dealers and used vehicle managers engineer an inventory that's better suited to attract buyers and meet today's more dynamic and fluid market demand.

This provides a natural advantage for velocity-minded dealers who use the Market Days Supply metric to stock their inventories. They don't have to spend as much on advertising to find buyers—the buyers will come to them. What's more, because these stores have the vehicles the market wants, there's less friction and pressure in the buying process. Customers have self-selected and landed on a dealership's vehicle because it's the one they want—not the one a used vehicle manager or salesperson needs to convince them to purchase.

If all this sounds almost magical, it's not. It's actually natural in an efficient market. Efficient markets reward the retailers who are the most proficient at identifying and taking advantage of opportunities. It also punishes the retailers who fail to dial into their respective markets.

Question 3: Why is the concept of a used car Market Days Supply seldom utilized?

There's an irony in the answer to this question. The fact is, dealerships are extremely familiar with the principles behind the Market Days Supply metric. In fact, their new vehicle inventory managers follow them every day when they order from their factories.

These managers use a variety of data sources, including their specialized knowledge of their own particular brand market as well as factory partners,

to know what's hot and what's not. It's this knowledge that gives them negotiation strength when a
factory rep pushes them to take additional orders
that they know won't fare well.

Likewise, these market-informed new vehicle inventory managers know when to take everything they
can get when there's high demand and low supply
for a particular model. Those are the units that
command MSRP and above, and allow salespeople
to politely smile when a customer asks about a
discount.

Now comes the twist: Dealers and used vehicle
managers typically don't follow these same supply and demand insights when they manage used
vehicle inventories. And who can blame them? The
old ways have worked for so long.

The difference now, of course, is that today's
more volatile and efficient used vehicle marketplace makes the traditional, less market-attuned
approach to inventory management more problematic. The composite we just reviewed shows
the advantage for stores that deploy velocity-based
metrics like Market Days Supply and those that
don't.

The contrast is striking. It should also serve as a
wake-up call to every dealership that still follows
traditional inventory management practices. Why

To me, the answer's a no-brainer. It's metrics like Market Days Supply that allow dealers to leverage the give-and-take power of today's more volatile and efficient used vehicle marketplace to their advantage.

would anyone who's invested millions in facilities and used vehicle inventory want to compete in a marketplace that punishes mistakes with anything less than the most up-to-date market information, such as Market Days Supply, to guide their decisions?

To me, the answer's a no-brainer. It's metrics like Market Days Supply that allow dealers to leverage the give-and-take power of today's more volatile and efficient used vehicle marketplace to their advantage.

It should be clear from this review of the Market Days Supply metric that becoming more attuned to the used vehicle marketplace, for any dealer or used vehicle manager, offers a better way to drive used vehicle inventory stocking decisions than the guesswork and historical brand-reflexive approaches our industry has relied on in the past.

Let's take another look at our three-store composite and ponder the question: Which store would you rather be—the one that benefits from a steady stream of customers because you've done the up-front, metric-enhanced homework to acquire vehicles your market wants, or the store that relies on traditional practices and wonders why Dealer Joe up the street is doing so well?

"PAINT" METRIC 2:
PRICE TO MARKET

In writing this chapter, I was torn between being brief versus really getting into the nuts and bolts of velocity pricing. Feel free to take a quick read and come back later. As we all know, pricing is not something that we can or should take lightly.

When it comes to pricing vehicles, there are two key features of today's more efficient and volatile marketplace that many traditional dealers and used vehicle managers often misunderstand.

The first is that they are most likely underestimating the borders of their market.

For Cary Donovan, who heads used vehicle operations for the Sam Swope Auto Group, the recognition of a new market area for his dealership group arrived in unlikely places—the local car wash and Starbucks coffee shop.

"The eye-opener for me came a few years ago when I would see vehicles with temporary tags from out of state," Donovan recalls.

At a Starbucks, he saw a black Lexus GX with an Illinois tag. "I complimented the guy for having a sharp-looking vehicle and asked if he lived in Illinois. 'No,' he says. 'My wife and I live in Louisville.' Oh, I'd say and ask if he'd looked for vehicles at Louisville dealers and visit any stores? 'No,' he says. 'We went online and found what we wanted on *Chicagocarsdirect.com.*'

"The next day I was at the car wash and saw a black BMW convertible with a Georgia tag. The guy lives in Louisville and found the car he wanted from a dealer in Atlanta. He bought the car and spent the weekend with friends before driving it home," Donovan says.

"It was like an out-of-body experience for me. I thought, 'Cary, what the heck have you been thinking? These are our customers telling you that they know what they want and will go find it outside Louisville if we don't have it priced competitively.'"

Donovan's wake-up call underscores one of the key
misconceptions that linger at traditional dealerships. With today's Internet-enabled buyers, the
market area for a dealership is a lot bigger than the
10-square mile radius that's detailed in most factory
franchise agreements. Therefore, when it comes to
pricing vehicles, the competition is more regional,
and sometimes national, for most franchised stores.

A second misconception held by many traditional
dealers and used vehicle managers is that they can
continue to use the time-honored practice of pricing vehicles by marking them up from their cost.

With today's Internet-driven used vehicle buyers,
this traditional pricing practice is often dangerous.
What if a used vehicle manager or buyer paid too
much to acquire a vehicle? Would today's price-
conscience buyers give that vehicle a look as they're
clicking through online listings?

The answer is that they might eyeball the traditional dealership's higher-priced unit, but they'd
likely skip past it to find a vehicle that's more
competitively priced.

It seems ironic that dealers price their used inventories in this way, because they would never allow
themselves to use the pricing practices of placing a
standard transaction mark-up on their new vehicle
inventories. If they purchased a hot new vehicle

from the factory that would command a premium asking price, they would price it above the standard mark-up.

The converse is also true: If new vehicles were selling for less than invoice pricing, dealers would not mark up the unit from invoice and advertise it to the world at or near MSRP.

But this, in effect, is how dealers and used vehicle managers have long established their retail asking prices for their used vehicles.

HOW THE PRICE TO MARKET METRIC WORKS

The Price to Market metric offers our industry's first-ever, real-time strategy to help dealers and used vehicle managers set competitive, profit-minded retail asking prices for their used vehicles.

Price to Market

DEFINITION:

How your vehicles are priced relative to other identically equipped vehicles in your market

The Price to Market metric provides this market intelligence by comparing the average retail asking prices for identically equipped, competing vehicles in a dealer's marketplace.

Example: If a dealership has a vehicle priced at $10,000, and the average retail asking price for identically equipped, competing units is $9,500, the Price to Market is 105%. Likewise, if the price on this same vehicle is $9,000, its Price to Market is 95%.

I recognize, out of the gate, that the Price to Market metric may seem like a stretch for traditional dealers and used vehicle managers that are accustomed to marking up from cost and not considering these values.

Additionally, in the past, it's been impossible to assess how one vehicle compares against another in a market, due to the vast matrix of available trim and equipment configurations on a given make/ model. Traditional dealers and used vehicle managers have also long believed that every vehicle is unique, a mindset that raises suspicion when anyone like me claims that there's a way to show detailed same-same comparisons between vehicles.

But this is where advances in technology allow more market-attuned and vehicle-specific price-setting strategies.

Today's leading technology allows the gathering of pricing information on every used vehicle in a given market area and enables a series of cross-checks against, not just VINs, but also detailed equipment descriptions to assure dealers and used vehicle managers are comparing vehicles that are, in fact, same-same. It's simply not enough to perform-apple-to-apple comparisons. Today's market requires a Granny Smith-to-Granny Smith comparison. Dealers can now see exactly what vehicles compete for consumer attention in their markets in a manner that's much more efficient than scanning newspaper ads or driving a competitor's physical or virtual lot late at night.

The Price to Market metric is another powerful part of the toolkit that velocity dealers and used vehicle managers use to increase sales volumes and profitable through-put of their used vehicle inventories—particularly when coupled with the knowledge of hot-selling vehicles that comes following the Market Days Supply metric.

So what is the right way to use the Price to Market approach to maximize both volume and profitability? The answer is not to price all vehicles high for the first 30 days nor is it to price all vehicles low out of the gate. Rather, the answer is to *know* which vehicles can and should be priced high and to be reduced slowly, and which vehicles should be priced low and reduced rapidly. In order to *know*, consider the following two tactics.

First, it's critical to know the physical qualities and appeal of the vehicle. There is still a merchandising and emotional aspect to used vehicles. This simply must be considered when determining an optimal price strategy. Second, after you know the physical qualities and appeal of the vehicle, the only relevant remaining consideration is the Market Day Supply of the vehicle at that moment.

The key advantages for velocity stores that use the Price to Market and Market Days Supply metrics in tandem include:

- The ability to know when they can price above market averages, because their vehicle stands taller than the competition and merits a higher asking price;

- The knowledge of when to re-price their unit to meet shifts in market demand and supply;

- Up-to-the-minute awareness of their vehicle's competitive positioning in the market-place—an impressive nugget that dramatically changes the nature of their sales processes and corresponding customer behaviors;

- The insights needed to adjust pricing and manage profit expectations on individual units as they age to avoid wholesale losses.

None of these advantages are available to dealers and used vehicle managers who follow traditional best practices for two reasons:

Reason 1: Yesterday's inefficient used vehicle marketplace never required this level of pricing sophistication. Decision makers would mark up vehicles from what they paid and call it good. Buyers, meanwhile, had a harder time comparing one dealership's used vehicle asking price against another. So, even if a dealer set prices above the market, customers often didn't know it. And, if they did, the dealers and used vehicle managers had negotiation-savvy salespeople to convince customers to pay the higher price.

This entire pricing dynamic falls apart in today's more efficient, volatile, and Internet-driven used vehicle marketplace. Today's online-shopping customers *know* what constitutes a competitive price and they'll pay less attention to vehicles that strike them as too high for the market.

"Nobody knew whether a car was worth $10,000, $11,000 or $12,000 unless they absolutely shopped around," says dealer Clay Close. "Now it's altogether different. All the information is out there online."

> **Reason 2:** Because traditional dealers and used vehicle managers have not had to pay much attention to pricing, thanks to yesterday's inefficient market, they simply don't.

At most stores, the initial asking price that gets placed on a vehicle typically remains the same for 30 or 45 days, sometimes longer. Meanwhile, astute velocity dealers like Chris Irwin and Cary Donovan are making multiple prices changes every week—sometimes daily—on the same vehicles.

Donovan says he gained an appreciation for the necessity of these more market-attuned and frequent price changes from keeping his ear to the ground with customers and friends in Louisville.

"It dawned on me that the Price to Market and Market Days Supply metrics made a lot of sense when I realized how the calls I would get from friends who were buying vehicles had changed," he says. "In the past, they'd call me and ask what they should buy and pay.

"Now, when they call me, they say they're looking at a G35, white with a tan interior and X number of miles and they think the price should be $18,000," Donovan continues. "They're not asking me to tell them what the market is for the vehicle, they know the market because they've done their homework."

I like to say the Price to Market and Market Days Supply metrics give managers the ability to set used vehicle prices that are reflective of their respective markets, rather than reflexive to their acquisition costs.

The following composite shows how powerful the Price to Market metric, when combined with the Market Days Supply metric, can be for a velocity

dealer in comparison to more traditional dealerships in the same market area.

Days in Inventory	Key Metric	Velocity Dealer	Traditional Dealer #1	Traditional Dealer #2
1-30	Market Days Supply	32	67	114
	Price to Market	90%	108%	105%
31-60	Market Days Supply	34	73	104
	Price to Market	85%	105%	107%
61-90	Market Days Supply	–	76	87
	Price to Market	–	105%	110%

Let's take a closer look at what's happening at each
store as their respective vehicles age:

The 1- to 30-day Bucket: As we established in
the earlier section on Market Days Supply, the
velocity dealer is more effective at stocking the
vehicles that the marketplace craves. When
combined with the Price to Market metric, this
dealership is producing the equivalent of a double whammy: It not only has more in-demand
vehicles, it's pricing them more competitively.
The 90% Price to Market ratio for the velocity
dealer means that, on average, the store is pricing a vehicle with an average retail asking price
of $10,000 at $9,000.

This is similar to the dynamic we noted in our Market Days Supply discussion wherein today's more efficient marketplace rewards velocity dealers with the blessing of more buyers seeking out their inventory and the profits that come from selling more vehicles faster. When the velocity dealer adds competitive prices to its in-demand vehicles, it's almost like it can't lose.

Meanwhile, the traditional stores are pricing their vehicles at $10,800 and $10,500. They are also creating their own double whammy, but theirs has a less-positive outcome than their velocity competition. The traditional stores are far less likely to attract buyers given they stock vehicles with less market demand, and price them higher than the marketplace's retail asking price average.

In this critical first 30 days of a used vehicle's lifecycle, when units are at their freshest and dealers and used vehicle managers stand to gain the most return on their investment, which of the three stores is best positioned to sell more vehicles and do so more quickly?

The answer once again should be obvious—the velocity dealer offers the most compelling value proposition for potential buyers in the marketplace these three stores share.

The dynamics highlighted during the first 30 days in this composite square up precisely with the kind of pricing approaches that Chris Irwin deploys at his store.

When a vehicle's hot and fresh in his inventory, he wants to be positioned in a way that makes his vehicles more competitive and compelling than his competition's vehicles. "We want to be in the top 50 percent" with our initial pricing, Irwin says. "If I want or need to, I can get more aggressive with my pricing strategy."

> **The 31- to 60-day Bucket:** This inventory age tier is a critical one for any dealership. It's in this window that vehicles will typically reach their win or lose threshold. During this stage, dealers and used vehicle managers intuitively understand that holding costs have mounted, and the potential for profit on these vehicles has diminished.

It's this intuitive understanding that leads more astute dealers and used vehicle managers to typically begin to make pricing adjustments. These pricing tweaks are intended to drum up buyer interest and remove aging units more quickly from their inventories.

The composite shows that two of the three stores understand the confluence of rising costs and diminished profit potential that occurs in this bucket. The velocity dealer has adjusted the initial Price to Market (90%) downward to 85%. Traditional Dealer #1 has also made an adjustment, from 108% to 105%.

Meanwhile, the Price to Market for Traditional Dealer #2 is heading the other direction. Why? There are two likely causes—both of which belie managers who are either less attuned to their market or flat-out asleep at the switch:

1. The dealer and used vehicle manager at Traditional Store #2 have not made any pricing adjustments from the initial, mark-up from cost approach they used. In this instance, I would bet the dealer regards his operation as a new car store and, consequently, not even the used vehicle manager is truly worried about stocking and pricing used vehicles to sell quickly.

2. Management has made some pricing adjustments but the tweaks were not significant enough to change the downward direction of the Price to Market metric for their overall inventory. For example, they may have several big-dollar vehicles that they believe will command a high price if/when they find a buyer. They haven't touched the pricing on these units, given they hold fast to the "ass for every seat" axiom.

But as they sit on these units, the efficient marketplace moves like water finding a low point. The consequence is an inventory that's even more out

of line in this crucial 31- to 60-day bucket, competitively speaking, than the other competing stores
and their shared market.

It's also worth examining the size of the pricing
adjustment the velocity dealer makes during this
make-or-break 31- to 60-day bucket.

Given the 34-day Market Days Supply metric for
the velocity dealer, it's fair to say the store still has
"in demand" vehicles. Ostensibly, it doesn't need
to beat the market price any further than the 90%
Price to Market it set during the initial 30-day
bucket.

But the dealer and used vehicle manager dial in
an 85% Price to Market during the 31- to 60-day
bucket—a full 5 percent price drop.

Why? The dealer and used vehicle manager recognize the importance of a consistent application of
velocity-based principles. That is, the vehicles in this
31- to 60-day bucket are older and their ability to
deliver a return on investment has diminished.

So, the pricing adjustments reflect a belief that the
store needs to rid itself of these vehicles even more
quickly to make room for other units that offer a
greater likelihood of selling faster and delivering
a better return on investment. The result of this
thinking process is a downward pricing adjustment

that's almost twice as deep than its closest competitor (5% versus 3%).

Did this velocity dealer lose some money on these units that it cleared out in the 31- to 60-day window? I would suspect that it did, but these losses will be significantly less than the losses the competing stores will take as a result of stocking vehicles that are less in demand in the market and pricing them above the competition, even as they grow longer in tooth in inventory.

"When vehicles start to age, we take the mentality like the stock market. Our first loss is our best loss," Irwin says.

Tom Kelley, CEO of Kelley Automotive, a seven-store dealer group based in Fort Wayne, Ind., who follows velocity principles to sell 400 used vehicles a month, takes a similar view. "If I'm not losing a little bit here and there, I'm not doing my job," he says. "That's the nature of an efficient market."

Some velocity dealers like Jack Anderson question whether the price reduction to move vehicles at the 60-day mark is truly a loss.

At the 60-day mark, his managers re-price inventory to rank No. 1 in their market—a move that Anderson says virtually guarantees calls and buyer interest. "You may lose money at retail, but I'm still ahead when you add in the $750 average for

F&I, the service and parts, and the opportunity for repeat/referral business. I'll retail these vehicles unless a 'loss' is thousands of dollars."

> **The 61- to 90-day Bucket:** The story here's similar to what we've already seen in the preceding inventory age buckets—with a key exception for the velocity dealer. It has no vehicles in its inventory because it priced them aggressively and got rid of them by the 60-day mark.

Contrast this move-the-iron mentality with the two traditional stores. Traditional Store #1 has made no additional pricing adjustments in this bucket. It's a "hold our ground" decision that owes, I suspect, to the earlier decision to adjust prices when vehicles were in the 31- to 60-day bucket.

The dealer and used vehicle manager at Traditional Store #2, meanwhile, still appear to be missing the boat. Maybe they're both tied up on the phone trying to arrange pick-ups from their wholesale buyers and don't have time to make pricing adjustments that might give them an increasingly diminished shot at turning a profit on their used vehicles. Whatever the case, Traditional Dealership #2 is poised to lose out even more than either of its competitors.

As we look at the composite with the Market Days Supply and Price to Market comparisons between these three stores, let's again ask: Which of these stores is best positioned to attract customers and sell more vehicles at a faster rate?

Fine-Tuning the Price to Market Metric

Today's technology allows dealership personnel to massage and manage the Price to Market metric to meet the needs of their respective businesses[6].

Chris Irwin at Irwin Motors can set his Price to Market to achieve retail asking prices that place his vehicles in the top 50% of his marketplace. He says this is a starting point for most vehicles— middle ground that balances his interest in achieving an inventory turn and retaining a profit margin on each unit.

If there are 12 vehicles competing against the one he owns, Irwin can set his Price to Market metric to position the vehicle, price-wise, at 6 out of 12. Likewise, if Irwin's appraisers or buyers stretched to own a unit, he might set the metric to position the vehicle at 4 out of 12. He does this to account for a higher acquisition price and the unit's reduced potential to achieve his target profit margin.

For example, if there are 12 vehicles competing against the one he owns, Irwin can set his Price to

---

[6] The vAuto system allows this flexibility by rendering the Price to Market metric through a Price Rank, which shows how a vehicle's price stacks up against identically equipped, competing vehicles in a dealership's self-selected market area. Example: If a vehicle has 10 competing units, a Price Rank of 6 would mean the unit's pricing ranks sixth among the competitive set; a Price Rank of 1 would make it a price leader.

Market metric to position the vehicle, price-wise, at 6 out of 12. Likewise, if Irwin's appraisers or buyers stretched to own a unit, he might set the metric to position the vehicle at 4 out of 12. He does this to account for a higher acquisition price and the unit's reduced potential to achieve his target profit margin.

The decision effectively positions the vehicle to sell more quickly, and allows Irwin to replace it with another unit that may bring a better return on investment. "It's a piece of metal and it's money. You've got to keep them moving," he says. "We can't be emotionally attached to our merchandise."

But velocity dealers like Irwin may not always make that price-lowering adjustment, particularly if a vehicle's Market Days Supply metric is low and it still stands tall, even with a bit of inventory age.

In some ways, the Price to Market metric allows dealers to "eat their cake and have it too" if they are running a velocity used vehicle department.

"We can also choose when we want to make a bit more money because we own the right vehicle better," Irwin says. "The converse is also true. We can price vehicles with higher days supplies more aggressively to move them more quickly."

Enter the "art" of fine-tuning the Price to Market metric.

As with any metric, the Price to Market metric serves as a numeric, market data-based barometer of how a used vehicle compares price-wise against competing vehicles in a given market area. Within this metric, however, there's flexibility for decision makers to let their own market and paint expertise carry the day.

Here are two examples of this fine-tuning in action:

Recalibrating a dealer's market area. It's not uncommon for velocity dealers and used vehicle managers to review comparative vehicle prices at distances that run up to 250 miles from their stores. Today's technology allows this "pick your market reach" flexibility. These dealers will adjust this market area, depending on supply and demand dynamics. If a vehicle's hot, they might opt to sell it close to home while it's fresh in inventory, and then expand the radius to match prices in other markets to move the vehicle quickly as it ages.

"If we've got a small comparative sample size, we'll go out 100 miles to get our comparisons," Irwin says.

Likewise, dealers may go even further if a vehicle's a rare bird.

John Creran, general sales manager for Ramsey Nissan in Upper Saddle River, N.J., notes how he

couldn't find a unit comparable to the '02 Land
Rover Discovery he took in on a recent trade, and
therefore expanded his search for comparable units
to scan the U.S.

"There wasn't anything like it out there. This
vehicle was loaded. I put it on *eBay National* and it
sold," he says.

> **Adjusting pricing buckets.** The composite of
> three stores with the Market Days Supply and
> Price to Market metrics shows the metrics at
> 30-day inventory intervals. As managers begin
> to adopt and follow velocity principles for
> managing their used vehicle inventories, many
> choose to set their pricing on even shorter time-
> frames, typically in 15-day buckets.

"My turn has increased by changing to 15-day
buckets," Creran says. The reason: He's even more
dialed in to his market and can make more frequent and more precise pricing adjustments to sell
vehicles faster.

"When I look at the buckets, I ask 'how come this
car hasn't moved?'" he says. "If I know customers
touched the car, and there's nothing wrong with it,
I've got to address the price."

Used vehicle consultant Tommy Gibbs has long
advocated this kind of market-focused attention
to inventory pricing. He advocates a pricing model

that offers buckets to appeal to buyer interest and budgets. When coupled with paint-based metrics like Price to Market, this approach produces winning results—provided there's the kind of proper attention dealers like Creran and others apply.

"To maximize profits, pricing has to be done in a disciplined and controlled manner," Gibbs says. "It's not just something you do when you get around to it."

"PAINT" METRIC 3:
COST TO MARKET

When I discuss the three key paint metrics to drive velocity-minded used vehicle management, dealers and used vehicle managers quickly see the benefits of the Market Days Supply and Price to Market metrics.

It's a no-brainer to understand that competitively priced vehicles with high demand and low supply will be winners for any store. Any retailer of any product should recognize that.

But many dealers and used vehicle managers get stuck when they ponder the bigger, operational outcome of adopting these metrics at their stores: How in the world am I going to make any money by pricing vehicles aggressively to beat the competition?

The answer to this question comes with the third critical paint metric, Cost to Market. This metric did not exist when I was a dealer when I, too, managed cost to wholesale or water versus managing against the more significant and relevant value, the current market price.

Cost to Market allows dealers and used vehicle managers to base their wholesale acquisition cost thresholds on what a customer is likely to pay at retail, rather than what dealers are willing to pay at wholesale. It goes to the heart of a dysfunction that occurs today when dealers and used vehicle managers acquire vehicles with no consideration for whether the market will bear the wholesale costs they've paid.

"You have to adopt the mentality that it's worth what I can sell it for—not how much I have or might put in it," says Tom Kelley. "Sometimes you luck out and get a car cheap. So, do you sell the car cheap? No, you sell it for what it's worth. How much you put in a vehicle is immaterial. It's worth what a customer will pay."

Ironically, dealers understand the principles behind the Cost to Market metric when they acquire and price new vehicles. As we discussed earlier, they typically do not add in a mark-up from the invoice price they paid to their factory partners. They set the price based on what the market will bear.

The Cost to Market metric offers a way to take the same astute, market-based approach to determining what a used vehicle is worth when considering whether to acquire one at auction or trade-in.

The metric is the cost of a vehicle divided by the average retail selling price of identically equipped, competing vehicles in a dealership's market area. As noted, today's leading technology allows these market comparisons for identical, competing vehicles in a given market.

Cost to Market

DEFINITION:

A vehicle's cost divided by the average retail asking price of identically equipped competing vehicles in your market

So, if the cost of a vehicle is $7,500 and the average retail asking price is $10,000, the Cost to Market for that unit is 75 percent.

The upshot: If a dealership makes this acquisition, the store has a 25 percent margin to factor in costs for reconditioning and a gross profit target for that unit—based on real-time market data indicating what a consumer's likely to pay.

Given that our business typically operates on single-digit net profit margins, it seems that an initial 25 percent margin would be a good place to start a used vehicle's life cycle at a dealership.

Velocity dealers and used vehicle managers pay close attention to this metric because it offers a data-driven approach to establish buy lists and determine the right amount to pay for a vehicle by reverse-engineering the acquisition cost off the prevailing retail prices in the market.

The composite on the next page shows how the Cost to Market metric, when combined with the other two paint metrics of Market Days Supply and Price to Market, can create significant competitive advantages for the dealers and used vehicle managers who adopt these metrics as guides for a velocity-based approach to managing their used vehicle operations.

When I share this composite with dealers and used vehicle managers, some are quick to spot why the velocity-minded dealer is performing much better than its traditional-minded competitors.

In each of the inventory buckets, the velocity dealer is able to acquire their vehicles at Cost to Market ratios that are significantly lower than their tradi-

Days in Inventory	Key Metric	Velocity Dealer	Traditional Dealer #1	Traditional Dealer #2
1-30	Market Days Supply	32	67	114
	Price to Market	90%	108%	105%
	Cost to Market	70%	85%	90%
31-60	Market Days Supply	34	73	104
	Price to Market	85%	105%	107%
	Cost to Market	75%	90%	98%
61-90	Market Days Supply	–	76	87
	Price to Market	–	105%	110%
	Cost to Market	–	95%	104%

tional counterparts. Any retailer worth his or her salt should be able to make a good living selling a product that they can acquire for 15 percent to 20 percent less than the competition.

But then comes incredulity and even doubt: How are the velocity-based stores able to achieve these margins? It's impossible to find some vehicles at wholesale prices less than what we typically charge at retail, given the increased competition and wholesale pressure in today's used vehicle marketplace. How is a 5 percent, let alone a 15 percent, margin even possible?

The answers to these questions lie in the way that velocity dealerships go about sourcing and acquiring vehicles. Let's examine the elemental components:

Establishing a baseline wholesale acquisition cost. As many dealers and used vehicle managers know, this is an increasingly tricky proposition, whether it's at an auction or trade-in appraisal.

The reason this can be tricky is because today's more volatile used vehicle marketplace can trigger dramatic wholesale values swings in a heartbeat. Anyone who was around dealerships in the latter part of 2008 should know this.

Gas price swings and a troubled economy combined to effectively crush wholesale values on large trucks and SUVs, and it spurred a spike in wholesale values for more fuel-efficient vehicles.

Most dealers and used vehicle managers did their best to keep up. They consulted the wholesale price guides from Kelley, Black Book, NADA, and other sources. But they still found themselves facing problems with aging vehicles and wholesale losses.

This was due, in part, to the wholesale guides having trouble keeping up with the rapid price changes. In fact, it's this very breed of volatility that has spurred wholesale guide providers to step up the frequency of publishing used vehicle values in the past 12 to 18 months. In some cases, these wholesale guides are now offered daily or weekly, but they still may not accurately catch the in-the-moment swings in wholesale values that can and do occur, particularly at crowded auction lanes.

These are the reasons why velocity dealers and used vehicle managers switch to using the Cost to Market metric to determine how much a vehicle is worth at wholesale. They know the metric offers a constant, real-time read of a non-debatable data point: The average retail asking price of a vehicle in a given marketplace.

From there, these velocity dealers and used vehicle managers can reverse engineer what they'll pay to acquire a vehicle.

For example, let's say a dealer and used vehicle manager are considering whether they should acquire a '07 Honda Accord that has an average retail asking price of $15,767 for a vehicle with similar mileage. This figure is the starting point for calculating an acquisition price that's right for the store.

The dealer and used vehicle manager would first decide how aggressively they need to price this car based on its physical qualities, appeal, and, importantly, its Market Days Supply. For example let's say they decide they need to be in the top 10 cars in their market for similarly equipped '07 Honda Accords and that this requires that they need to price it at 95% of average market price. First, they would subtract the amount they expect to pay for reconditioning (say, $800) and the $2,000 gross profit from the asking price to arrive at an acquisition price of $12,179 (a 77% Cost to Market ratio).

If it's a trade-in, they'd send that figure to the desk. If it's an auction purchase, the dealer and used vehicle manager may go a step further, and set the ceiling on the acquisition price at $12,979 (determined by adjusting the gross profit expectation to roughly $1,200 and weighing the benefit of bringing a fast-moving unit into their inventory).

Exit Strategy

Avg. Market Price	$15,767
Adj % of Market X	95%

Asking Price	$ 14,979
Reconditioning	$ - 800
Profit Objective	$ -2,000

Appraised Value	**$ 12,179**

Now, let's contrast this market-attuned approach to establishing the right wholesale acquisition with what traditional dealers and used vehicle managers are likely to do.

As noted above, they'd potentially consult the wholesale value guides, but there's also a chance they might neglect the guides and go with their guts. Likewise, they might get caught up in the irrational exuberance at auction and pay more than they should—even if they knew the acquisition cost outpaced a wholesale value guide.

"I pity the poor guy who's only got a Black Book or other guide," says dealer Joe Kirby of Edd Kirby Adventure Chevrolet, Dalton, Georgia. "He's not going to know everything he needs to make a good decision."

In early fall 2009, Kirby and his buyer are walking out of auctions without buying any vehicles, a rare move that comes from knowing his Cost to Market thresholds on the units he might acquire for his store. "We've seen eight months of appreciating values," Kirby says. "That has not happened in the history of mankind."

Given these factors, the reverse engineer approach that velocity-minded dealers and used vehicle managers follow, based on the Cost to Market metric, is a far more reasonable, measured, and data-supported way to determine what wholesale price the store should pay for a given vehicle than traditional practices.

This approach to establishing what to pay is a key reason why the velocity dealer in the composite example is able to achieve a Cost to Market for its inventory that's far lower than the traditional-minded competition.

Sourcing vehicles. The traditional stores in our composite are likely to rely on one or two local auctions to source their vehicles. What's more, the used vehicle manager or buyer is probably accustomed to going to an auction only occasionally, perhaps once every two weeks— potentially more frequently at larger stores. (Remember, these stores have historically relied more on trade-ins than auctions to drive the bulk of their used vehicle inventories.)

Let's contrast this auction expertise with that of the buyers and used vehicle managers at velocity stores where, by definition, they need to continually feed their fast-turning inventories:

- It's not uncommon for these stores to have inventory specialists who spend 80 percent of their time scouring auction run lists to find vehicles that fit their Market Days Supply parameters.

- They fly two to three days a week to the auctions (sometimes with airfare and hotel expenses paid by the auctions themselves, thanks to their volume of business) with up-front knowledge of the specific auction lanes and run times for the vehicles they want. Likewise, they take full advantage of the online sales offered by Manheim, ADESA, Openlane, and factory sales.

- They know when they can pay all day long and when to let a vehicle go because the bidding goes well beyond the Cost to Market metric they calculated before they left the store.

- They know which auctions offer better acquisition price points based on specific vehicle segments. Example: Southeast auctions appear better for high-lines than other locations.

- They know the auctions that typically offer vehicles in the best condition and offer the best prospect for a low reconditioning expense. Example: It's not at Midwest auctions like those in Detroit and Chicago where winter driving conditions almost guarantee paint and bodywork in the recon line.

- They've arranged transports for the vehicles they plan to purchase in advance, or they've invested in their own transports, thereby shortening the time and expense required to get the vehicles back to their stores.

- They have additional opportunities to bid on vehicle batches that sell outside the auctions.

I've analyzed the cumulative effect of these more efficient sourcing tactics and believe they account for a full 5 percent of the Cost to Market differential noted in the three-store composite.

Our industry has long believed that someone who holds the title of used vehicle manager necessarily makes a good buyer. The examples I've shared here, which reflect the real-life experiences that occur every day at velocity dealerships, underscore that this belief needs revisiting.

Reconditioning Expenses. Two blessings that flow from a velocity-minded approach to managing used vehicle operations are the efficiencies and economies of scale that result from moving a higher number of vehicles through the used vehicle department. This plays out in a profound way when it comes to reconditioning vehicles.

Velocity-minded dealers have established processes that shorten the time it takes to move a vehicle from the transport to the reconditioning/detailing department and to the front line in just two or three days. It's not uncommon for more traditional stores to see a week or more pass before a vehicle is ready for retail.

With volatile wholesale values and holding costs increasing, these delays can be costly for stores that fail to speed up their reconditioning turn times.

Likewise, velocity dealers pay less for oil filters, fenders, belts, fluids, windshields, and the cleaning products they use to get vehicles reconditioned and ready for retail. Or they pay less on a per-vehicle basis to the vendors that do this work for them. No dealer or used vehicle manager would argue that it costs less per vehicle to recondition 200 vehicles than 20.

Such economies of scale are another key reason why the Cost to Market metric in the three-store composite is lower for the velocity store than its traditional-minded competitors.

Taken together, the kinds of efficiencies that velocity dealerships are able to achieve—from setting a reliable benchmark on what they should pay to acquire a vehicle to achieving economies of scale in reconditioning—account for the margin advantage these stores retain over their competition.

When I share this overview of the Cost to Market metric, and explain why velocity dealerships are able to achieve a cost advantage compared to their competitors, dealers and used vehicle managers begin to get the picture.

In essence, it reflects one of life's key blessings and truths: The more you do something, the better you'll get at it.

FINE-TUNING THE COST TO MARKET METRIC

Similar to the Price to Market metric, the Cost to Market metric is only a benchmark. There are definitely occasions when velocity dealers and used vehicle managers may want to hedge their bets to suit other business purposes.

For example, Tom Kelley shares an example of a loyal customer who traded in a '06 Cadillac STS with 11,000 miles. The vehicle was in like-new condition—a well-maintained unit with a 70-year-old single owner. The store's target Cost to Market (80 percent) pegged the trade-in value at $17,500.

But Kelley paid $19,500 to own the unit. Why? It helped him book a new car deal for a loyal customer and his examination of the competitive data on the vAuto system showed the vehicle was a true-blue creampuff.

"I know I can get more than $20,000 for the car," says Kelley, who acknowledges the front-end gross of the retail deal may be thinner than he'd get if he'd been stricter about sticking to the Cost to Market metric. But, in this instance, he's taking the gamble.

"I'm less concerned about going outside the metric parameters on this car. You can't get killed on a car like that with 11,000 miles," he says.

Sometimes, as Kelley relates, it may make sense to put the Cost to Market metric aside. The key, however, is making sure such a decision follows a careful assessment of the potential risks and rewards of doing so—which one can only truly assess by evaluating the Market Days Supply and Price to Market metrics on a vehicle in tandem with the Cost to Market metric.

I would say Kelley made the right call. He checked the market, assessed the good will he'd get from a loyal customer, the benefit of a new car deal, and his ability to retail the STS, even with a thinner margin. Given that his stores turn their inventory nearly 18 times a year, it's a fair bet that STS won't be around very long on his lot.

How might this deal have gone at another, more traditional dealership?

They probably would have paid the $19,500, given the seller is a loyal customer. Then, the dealer and used vehicle manager would likely have reflexively placed a $4,000 mark-up on the unit—putting it on the market at $23,500.

The store *may* find a buyer at that price, but I would be willing to bet good money that this store will spend more time waiting for this buyer than the one who's likely to hop online, see the unit priced more competitively at Kelley's store, and snap it up.

In the end, who's made the more profitable deal?

I would suggest it's Kelley, who's already bought and sold at least one other vehicle with the money

he initially invested in the '06 STS in the time
it took the traditional store to turn its initial
investment.

VELOCITY METRICS AND THE ROAD AHEAD

There's an axiom in business that one should
always put a positive spin on things—even if something is undeniably negative.

There's no sense mincing words here: Adopting a
velocity-based philosophy and effectively using the
"paint" metrics described in these chapters—Market
Days Supply, Price to Market and Cost to Market—
to manage used vehicle operations won't work for
every dealership.

I'm not saying they *can't* work, because I believe
wholeheartedly that they do. I'm just saying that
the transition to a velocity-based philosophy and
metrics-minded management approach is not easy.
This stuff's new. It runs counter to what most dealers and used vehicle managers consider the right
thing to do.

We'll see more of that in the next chapter.

I'll share why an increasing number of dealers are
giving up their long-held obsession with uber per
vehicle gross on used cars, and focusing more on
total gross, storewide net profits, and more efficient

operations. We'll learn how these stores are changing job descriptions and creating new ones to get the jobs of online merchandising, sourcing, and selling vehicles done with more effectiveness and proficiency. We'll also examine how difficult it is to make this critical transition, and why some dealers and used vehicle managers don't make the cut.

It's an exciting story. I can't wait to tell it.

"PAINT-BASED" PROCESSES
AND PRESSURE POINTS

I want to be clear about something—I didn't invent velocity-based management principles.

The last thing I want or need is an "Al Gore[7]"-like rap against me. I may be one of the first in our industry to openly and publicly advocate for using market-based velocity principles for managing used vehicle departments. But these management principles are as old as the financial hills. They've been in use for years in stock and commodity markets as well as in a host of other retail-focused industries.

---

[7]http://www.snopes.com/quotes/internet.asp

Even so, these concepts are new and different for most traditional dealers and used vehicle managers. Interestingly, I'm not the only person in automotive retailing who thinks this is a far better way to run a used vehicle business in today's more volatile, efficient, and Internet-enabled used vehicle marketplace than traditional best practices.

Take a peek at how the 30-something-year-old founders of online auto retailing powerhouse Texas Direct think about their business—culled from their book, *0 to 60*:

> *"The Internet market is different than what most dealers are used to. The books are of little use; the only index that matters is the global market. The only way to know the market is to be buying and selling in it, day in and day out. Will the market bear a profit on a certain vehicle at a given purchase price? If so, then buy. If not, then don't buy.[8]"*

> *"By being as fast as possible, you protect yourself from market fluctuations. It's one thing to buy something and sell it for a profit. It's another to use that same money twice in one month and make a profit twice. We turn our inventory of 400 vehicles more than once a month. [9]"*

---

[8] *0 to 60*, p. 36.
[9] *Ibid*, p. 69..

I share this excerpt for a couple of key reasons:

> First, the guys at Texas Direct are eating the
> lunches of many franchised dealers and used
> vehicle managers—and not just in Texas. The
> outfit's success comes from buying and sell-
> ing vehicles across the country. Customers fly
> in from all corners to take delivery of vehicles
> they've purchased. They are keen competitors.

> Secondly, the fact that two young guys, with no
> prior experience in auto retailing and a com-
> paratively scant brick-and-mortar investment,
> have crafted a 400-plus-per-month sales success
> based on velocity-like principles should be a sig-
> nificant wake-up call for traditional dealerships.

It's clear that technology and data-driven insights
about the market, as well as a need for inventory
turn speed, serve as the underlying foundation of
the Texas Direct business model. That's velocity,
baby, and it's working wonders for their operation.
The young entrepreneurs at Texas Direct created
and crafted their velocity-minded operation sans
any regard for traditional used vehicle management best practices. In fact, judging from their
book, they basically assessed those best practices
and decided on a different direction. To them, the
way we've long managed used vehicle operations is
too inefficient and dealer-centric to work in today's
marketplace.

That's bad news for traditional dealers and used vehicle managers. Why? Because it underscores how much work it takes to transform long-standing culture and processes into the velocity-based practices we discussed in the past three chapters.

This chapter seeks to ease this important transition. It focuses on some of the most critical flashpoints that occur as dealers and used vehicle managers adopt velocity-based paint metrics and management principles. These pressure points crop up in every department that touches a used vehicle during its life cycle, and they create ongoing "out with the old, and in with the new" struggles at every store that walks this bold new path.

In some ways, the cultural clashes that occur between velocity-based and traditional used vehicle best practices are essentially battles for greater efficiencies. With velocity-based management principles, speed and turn are key elements of this highly time-sensitive approach. With traditional best practices, speed and turn play little, if any, role, and time is an ally, not an enemy.

So with the backdrop of industry newbies capitalizing on the benefits that velocity-based management offers in today's more volatile and efficient used vehicle marketplace, let's examine the areas that give dealerships that have adopted this new mindset the most trouble.

Get Off the Gross and Go with 'Net'

The controller and accounting team of a South Carolina-based dealer group were at a loss as to why one of its stores consistently grew net profits while front-end gross profits were softer than they'd been in years past.

"It's because of an old school mentality that focuses on gross," says the store's GM, who, since adopting a velocity-based approach to management has doubled the store's used vehicle sales volume to 200-plus in six months. "They couldn't understand how I was making so much net profit when my grosses were lower."

The store's front-end gross profit average on used vehicles hovers around $1,200. But as the GM is quick to note, that's only a part of the profit picture at his store. The following are examples of improvements experienced since implementing velocity-based management principles:

- Service revenues from reconditioning work have tripled to more than $600,000 in the first three months. The increase owes to the greater number of used vehicles that now need reconditioning work. "We're running 300 units a month through service to sell 200," the GM says.

- F&I penetration has increased to 150 percent, up from 125 percent. The store is looking to hire additional F&I managers.

- The store's new vehicle sales volume is increasing, albeit at a slower clip than usual due to high unemployment in the region. Still, the GM says, "we're doing more deals because we can pony up at the pump on trades."

Such is the total profit picture at dealerships that adopt a velocity-based management philosophy and paint metrics to run used vehicle operations. It's more about net profit across multiple dealership departments than average gross profit on a retailed unit (PVR).

"I'm all about running my dealership based on net, not gross," says Bill Pearson. "Net profit matters most."

"You absolutely have to let go of gross as part of your decision-making," echoes John Malishenko. "It must shift to turn and net profits. It's a leap of faith because it's totally contrary."

Indeed, it is. This velocity-based mentality is not easy to achieve at stores where traditional dealers and used vehicle managers have long focused on PVR as an elemental read on whether a used vehicle department is healthy or not.

Even velocity dealers and used vehicle managers who have achieved improvements in net profits across multiple departments still have to contend with owners, partners, and parents who believe they'd make even more money if they just ratcheted up gross profits a bit more.

"It's difficult for my dad and partner," says dealer Dan Sunderland at Sun Motor Cars, Mechanicsburg, Pa. "If we're making $2,400 front-end gross on a car, and we used to make $3,500, he thinks we're leaving $1,100 on the table. I can't look him straight in the eye and say that's not sometimes the case.

"But if you add the additional gross in fixed operations, the grosses from buying and selling more vehicles from manufacturer programs, and the reduction in wholesales losses, we are making more money. But the money's in different pockets," Sunderland says.

The challenge for velocity dealerships like Sun Motor Cars is balancing the gross profit expectations against the need to turn inventory. This ever-important balancing act is typically achieved by vectoring the Market Days Supply, Price to Market and Cost to Market metrics to get the best shot at a gross profit while a vehicle is freshest in inventory.

Remember Chris Irwin's strategy of being in the middle, price-wise, when a vehicle hits his lot for retail? He aims for his best gross profit out of the gate, and dials back expectations as vehicles age. Sometimes, given market data, he may come out as a price leader because it's necessary to move the vehicle fast, given a weaker initial profit position.

Even then he's focused on turn and overall gross for the used vehicle department, not PVR.

Some traditional dealers and used vehicle managers simply can't get off the PVR juice. They'll hear that gross profits on individual deals don't matter as much as they used to and they'll hit a mental wall.

It's understandable because it's very difficult to let go of practices and beliefs that have served us all well for years.

But the dismissal of velocity metrics and management principles misses some key benefits that may not be readily apparent. These benefits are a natural bi-product of the application of a velocity-based philosophy and gain momentum as they are utilized.

Together with the storewide efficiencies and net profit gains that flow from adopting velocity principles, these benefits demonstrate that once dealers and used vehicle managers put the efficiency-fueled velocity train on its tracks, it can become an express line to used vehicle success.

Benefit 1: Inventory that's innately ready to move. Velocity dealers and used vehicle managers are more likely to stock vehicles with favorable Market Days Supply metrics. So, in some ways, by implementing the velocity management strategies the pressure to move inventory is already reduced because these store buy the right vehicles.

What's more, because these vehicles are in demand, customers seek out the dealers who sell them. This translates to velocity dealers and used vehicle managers dumping traditional advertising costs altogether—a cost reduction that goes straight to the bottom line. Of course, this savings won't show up on a PVR report, but it'll fatten up the department's net profit picture.

Benefit 2: Less pressure on gross at point of sale. We all know what happens with hot new vehicles that command prices above MSRP. Customers know they're paying a premium to get a vehicle ahead of their neighbors. They may inquire about a discount, but a little push-back from salespeople generally results in customers ponying up to pay the premium. The same dynamic is true at velocity stores where they use the Market Days Supply and Price to Market metrics effectively. Customers have done their shopping online; they arrived on a unit because it represents a good value compared to identically equipped, competing vehicles.

In most cases, their efforts to negotiate for a
discount really amount to testing a dealership
only to check if it is strong and transparent
enough to stand behind its market-based pricing. "You don't have to be the cheapest to sell
today's price-savvy customers," is a comment I
hear all the time. And it's true. Velocity dealers
know when vehicles can command big grosses,
and they know when leaner margins are more
appropriate, given market dynamics. All they're
doing is linking their pricing decisions to match
what customers already know. The end result is
a greater number of deals with less negotiation
and fewer discounts to arrive at a selling price
in which both sides walk away winners.

"When customers come to us, they're ready," says
Steve Barnes, used vehicle manager at Sun. "It's
amazing. They know the car. They know the price.
If we give up any money during negotiations, it's
only a few hundred dollars from our price. It's rare
to have a long, grinding negotiation on a deal."

When the Market Days Supply and Price to Market
metrics are properly aligned, the phones ring at
velocity stores. As previously stated, the advertising
savings these stores achieve goes straight to the bottom line—and they'll go unnoticed by traditional
dealers and used vehicle managers who focus solely
on PVR.

Benefit 3: The ability to dial in for dollars. It'd be an interesting exercise to see how much time and productivity is lost at traditional dealerships as they wait for customers to show up and land on a used vehicle that's been priced to achieve a fantasy mark-up. In these environments, it's not uncommon for a salesperson who achieves 10 to 15 sales a month to be regarded as a good seller.

At some velocity dealerships, however, 10 units a month is the price of entry for salespeople. As we'll discuss shortly, pay plans at velocity stores are structured for salespeople to average 15 to 20 units a month—with good sellers hitting 25-plus deals.

The velocity-based metrics and management principles support this level of proficiency and productivity because dealers and used vehicle managers are able to adjust their prices when needed to bring in customers. The expertise they develop for this move the market technique is uncanny. Some even know the time and day of the week that will result in more phone calls and foot traffic as a result of pinpoint price changes.

Craig Belowski says Thursday price changes make for a profitable weekend. He adds that his attention to market-based pricing gives him a competitive edge.

"I'm checking our pricing every day. Nobody else around here is doing that," says Belowski, whose store averages 140 units a month and consistently ranks as a top regional Toyota certified pre-owned retailer.

I would urge traditional dealers and used vehicle managers to "get off the gross and go with 'net.'" It's a significant change, for sure, but the benefits strike me as far better than those that result from retaining traditional best practices in today's more efficient and volatile used vehicle marketplace.

IT'S A SOURCING PROBLEM, NOT A SHORTAGE

I've had dozens of conversations about what some dealers and used vehicle managers believe is a shortage of used vehicles.

> *"We can't find the vehicles we need at prices we can afford to pay."*

> *"We have to pay the same at wholesale as we charge at retail."*

When we peel back the layers of this onion, it becomes clear to me that these dealers and used vehicle managers are running up against a problem other than a shortage of vehicles. The vehicles with low Market Days Supply are out there—but they're

A Volume-based Velocity Payplan

It's not uncommon for velocity-minded dealerships to see sales volumes increases create problems with commission-based compensation plans for salespeople.

It's to be expected as salespeople do more deals and traditional, 25 percent commission-based pay plans start eating away at profitability for a department that's focused on turn and net rather than PVR.

Here's how one velocity-minded dealer solved the problem—a pay plan that keeps his compensation costs at a respectable 22 percent and his salespeople earning a good living.

The plan gives a $2,000/month base, with the following bonuses:

6 units sold by the 15th:	$200
10 units a month:	$500
15 units a month:	$500
@ 5 add'l units:	$500

In addition, the store pays up to 4 percent commission on total F&I dollars that flow from a salesperson's deals, based on $10,000 increments (*e.g.*, $0-$10,000 = 1 percent).

The dealer expects salespeople to do at least 10 deals a month or they'll be looking for another job.

The keys here are the initial spiff to spur front-of-month sales and the incentive to ensure salespeople set up potential F&I penetrations. It's important to underscore the F&I office's value early on with today's customers, whose online shopping exposes them to a variety of do-it-yourself financing and warranty options.

not necessarily available at the local auctions traditional dealers and used vehicle managers have relied on in the past.

The real problem is that many dealers and used vehicle managers, including some that have adopted velocity-based management principles, now have to work harder to find the vehicles they need to feed their inventories.

"The cars are out there, but they're not at the traditional places we've gone to in the past," says velocity-minded dealer Keith Kocourek of Kocourek Chevrolet, Wausau, Wis. "They're also not the traditional cars we've had in the past."

Another problem arrives when velocity dealers and used vehicle managers find the vehicles that fit their Market Days Supply metric: they aren't the only ones who want to buy them, translating to purchase prices that often go north of the desired acquisition prices.

The GM for the South Carolina store says he's seen his Cost to Market climb from 72 percent to 80 percent in 2009 as a result of greater pressure and demand for auction vehicles. "It hurts the margin and gross, but I think it will get better," he says.

Adam Simms, dealer/owner of Toyota Sunnyvale (Calif.), takes a similar view. "It's ridiculous to say there's a shortage when at any given time, there are nearly 3 million used vehicles in some stage of preparation or sale," says Simms, noting the nation's $40 million annual used vehicle sales tally. "You can always buy the cars, but you have to adjust your expectations for your margin. I still buy the cars because I want to maintain velocity and be the only guy who has them."

This breed of confidence comes from the fact that Simms knows his acquisition, stocking, and pricing strategy is more market-attuned than his traditional-minded competitors. His store currently sells about 220 used units a month and he's planning for additional growth.

Simms concedes that the market in 2009 marks "a period of time when margins may well be thinner" and every store must work harder to proficiently acquire vehicles—and know when to hold, fold, or buy the units they seek.

Here's a look at how some velocity dealers address the challenge of sourcing the vehicles they need at the price that's right for their stores:

Designate an inventory specialist(s). "Hey, Hoss. What can you do for me on that '07 Escalade?"

That's Kyle Cornwell on the horn with an auction rep, trying to resolve a problem with a vehicle that got damaged in transport. So it goes at the central-

ized appraisal and buying office at Sam Swope
Auto Group, Louisville, Ky.

"I call Kyle 'The Hammer,'" says Burnell King,
Cornwell's partner in the centralized appraisal and
buying office at the dealer group. "I just give him a
phone number and the problem gets taken care of."

Arbitrations are a part of life here, where a majority
of the vehicles that fuel Swope's 700-unit monthly
used vehicle sales volume get purchased online.
King estimates he and Cornwell average about 25
vehicle buys a day, plus they handle appraisals for
group stores.

King and Cornwell are grinders. They work from 9
a.m. to 9 p.m. five days a week and a half-day on
Saturdays, using a host of technology and tools to
buy and appraise vehicles. An open box of Raisin
Bran cereal on the top of a small refrigerator serves
as testimony that these guys are glued to their computers and telephones, making deals and moving
metal.

"We don't really have time for lunch," King
explains. "That's when auctions are at their peak.
And, we're also trying to slim down a bit."

Each morning this tandem reviews buy lists pre-
pared the night before from reviews of auction
run sheets and velocity metrics. For the next seven
hours, King and Cornwell are monitoring auction

sales, making bids, checking proxy bids, and scouring for vehicles.

They tend to buy in small batches versus truckloads to ensure they're getting vehicles that match up squarely with the Market Days Supply, Price to Market, and Cost to Market metrics for the stores they serve. "We do the same amount of up-front work to purchase 3 vehicles as we do 30," King says. "If we need 3 vehicles, and an auction has 300, we have to review them all."

The smaller-batch purchases also help speed up the time it takes to transport vehicles back to Swope— a critical aspect of the efficiency-focused sourcing. "The challenging thing is that these vehicles hit the DMS as soon as we buy them," King says. "That's when the clock starts ticking."

In my travels around the country, the centralized appraisal and buying operation at Swope is one of the most efficient sourcing operations I've had the pleasure to visit. It's this kind of sourcing proficiency and efficiency that's necessary for dealerships to thrive in today's used vehicle marketplace.

The work King and Cornwell do looks nothing like the auction fishing trips that many traditional dealers and used vehicle managers still rely on to source vehicles. King and Cornwell remind me of snipers: Armed with buy sheets derived from calibrating auction run lists and their velocity metrics, they know exactly when to pull the trigger and when to hold their fire.

"We source vehicles the same way we sell—with a lot of information about our market," says Cary Donovan, who set up the centralized office as a way to streamline sourcing and create a more cost-efficient and aggressive method for feeding his velocity-focused used vehicle operation. "Their job boils down to one thing—putting the right price on every car. They both know their stuff and do it extremely well."

From my observations, I would have to agree. It's pretty easy to tell, after a short visit to King and Cornwell's shared office, that they're the right guys for the job.

King, who spent about six years on the road buying vehicles for CarMax before joining Swope, says the market-driven metrics and methods they follow at Swope gives him more latitude to exercise his paint skills.

"You get to think a little more and put your own spin on things," King says. "CarMax is more robotic. You work with what's put in front of you."

Get creative. In addition to bringing on inventory specialists and going beyond local and familiar auctions, dealers like the Swope Auto Group are making house calls to acquire vehicles. In 2009,

Donovan launched a "We Pay Cash For Cars" effort that now brings in 20 to 25 units a month from customers the store probably would not have seen without the program. Cornwell and King's office runs the program and "it creates a natural flow of traffic," King says. "People who have a car to sell generally need a car, too."

The program does mean Swope pays for rough cars that go immediately to wholesale. But, with the market-based metrics to set the right purchase price, "it's a profit center if it goes wholesale or retail," King says.

The West Herr Automotive Group has also found that purchasing cars from customers can be a helpful way to source and sell vehicles, says Jack Anderson. In spring 2009, the group began offering a program to help customers sell their vehicles online. The store would help prep descriptions and photos and offer an appraisal.

In most cases, the customers simply took the appraisal offer and the dealership sourced another vehicle. "It's not high pressure and most customers appreciate the fact that we offer fair appraisals," says Anderson, who estimates about half of these customers wound up purchasing a used vehicle to replace the one they sold. In the fall of 2009, the company plans to market and launch the program more aggressively.

"You can't put all your eggs in one basket when it comes to sourcing," Anderson adds.

Dealership consultant Steve Nickelson agrees. He believes such creative sourcing approaches are critical, given greater demand at wholesale for vehicles.

"The dealerships that don't re-think sourcing and stick to the traditional mode of sending somebody to the auction to raise their hand, are going to be at a significant disadvantage," he says. "Having a variety of sourcing options will be critical going forward."

Avoid the appraisal games on trades. Dealer Jon Whitman says today's technology allows him to show customers why the store can only pay a certain dollar amount for a vehicle, rather than a figure that either over-allows or under-allows on a given trade. "We knew a vehicle was worth $10,000 and we'd allow $11,000 for some customers all the time," he says.

This traditional practice may be an occasional necessity to satisfy loyal customers or close a new vehicle deal. He notes it must be a decision that's informed with an honest assessment of Cost to Market and Price to Market metrics to ensure the vehicle doesn't end up priced too high for the market to accommodate the over-allowance.

"We make sure the person who appraises the car doesn't price the car," says John Malishenko. "You have to take any biases and ego out of the decision-making and still use common sense."

The upshot of today's sourcing game is that it's more difficult and challenging than ever before. It requires an investment of time, money and resources to do the job proficiently and to set the stage for a positive return on investment for every vehicle a store acquires.

This is a far cry from the gut-based buying decisions and wasted time that's typical of the way most traditional dealers and used vehicle mangers sought out used vehicle inventory—if they did it at all.

TURNING WRENCHES, TURNING CARS

Another key challenge that velocity-minded dealers and used vehicle managers confront early on in their journey to create a fast-turning inventory is ensuring that all used vehicles get attention and priority in their service departments.

Make no mistake: This shift amounts to a cultural change at most dealerships and it requires up-front effort to ensure service directors, advisors, and technicians all understand that every vehicle slated for reconditioning represents an investment of the dealership's money, and that any delay—no matter the cause—crimps the store's ability to generate the maximum return on investment on any given unit.

For example, if a store's average days-in-inventory runs 17-25 days, a benchmark that's fairly common at velocity-minded stores, a 5-, 6- or 7-day lag in service hampers profitability. Such lags can cut as much as 50 percent of the time a vehicle lives in the 15-day buckets many velocity-minded stores use for their retail pricing strategies. If that occurs, it absolutely undermines the dealership's potential to garner a maximum level of profit.

From my conversations with velocity dealers, a "carrot and carrot" approach to achieving a shared understanding that time is of the essence in service seems to work best. That is, it's more effective to foster a culture of collaboration and shared goals than one that relies on the "stick" of penalties and charges to the service department for delays.

One of the key factors in achieving buy-in in service is the straight-up fact that everyone in the shop stands to benefit from a velocity-based approach. Paychecks will get fatter for service teams that accommodate the incremental influx of work.

The next step is a process that ensures the prioritization and turn for vehicles.

The GM at the South Carolina store aims for a three-day timeframe to complete all reconditioning work (the third day goes to paint/body work if it's needed). He tracks the progress "like crazy" using a status board posted in the service department. He also discusses vehicle status daily with the service manager to address any issues, such as delays for parts, costs that run north of preliminary estimates, etc., that inevitably come up.

"It's very collaborative," he says. "Everybody has to play their position."

Bill Pearson sets an even more aggressive expectation for his reconditioning turn: Within 48 to 72 hours, his vehicles are detailed, reconditioned, and loaded up to his online listings. His detailing manager handles the photos and gets paid based on meeting Pearson's goals for getting the vehicle ready for sale.

"It's all about being efficient and making sure everybody understands that," Pearson says.

Malishenko says he found success at building service department buy-in by empowering his team members to devise the best ways to ensure speedy through-put of used vehicles. The buy-in flowed from an education and training process that came without mandates. In effect, it let GMs at stores work with their service departments to devise the best ways to ensure vehicles didn't suffer from time delays.

"We wanted this change to be their idea," he says. "We took our time, and had hours and hours of dialogue. To be successful, it has to be a holistic thing that everybody understands—the service manager, the detail manager, the reconditioning technicians, the salespeople, and the new and used car managers."

The key take-away is that a velocity-minded approach requires astute management of expectations in service and other departments to ensure a storewide focus on efficient movement of used vehicles through their lifecycle.

Along the path of this important, time-is-critical cultural shift for reconditioning work, it's not uncommon for velocity stores to encounter another issue: Just how much is the correct amount to pay to get a vehicle ready for sale?

The answer to this question varies, depending on the vehicle. Velocity dealers and used vehicle managers share a wide range of average reconditioning costs, from $400 to $2,000.

The disparity flows from their business models: Are they trying to be price leaders in the market? If so, the average reconditioning will likely run closer to the $400 average. Are they aiming to be competitive while providing a vehicle that may command a higher mark-up? If so, the store will likely fall closer to the $2,000 average.

Such considerations have given rise to what West Herr Automotive Group calls its value vehicles. These are units—denoted by a green-colored sticker—that may have some cosmetic flaws, but offer a good buy for customers. Anderson says the approach helps mitigate situations where the "money we spend to make a car look good" may not be best for positioning the vehicle competitively in the market.

Of course, factory certification programs add another layer of complexity to the reconditioning equation. By their nature, the reconditioning costs for these vehicles will be higher. The question for dealers and used vehicle managers is how much higher should these reconditioning costs be? And, if they invest this money, will it attract customers willing to pay the premium?

At Acton Toyota, Craig Belowski says the difference in reconditioning costs between certified and non-certified vehicles runs between $300 and $400. The trick, he says, is studying the market to know what vehicles will command a better premium than others with the CPO badge.

For example, he says a loaded Sienna AWD van might command a $2,000 premium, while a less

well-equipped Camry LE might only add $500.
Likewise, certification on a '09 Camry program car
might not matter as much as on an older vehicle.

HERE ARE SOME KEY NOTES ON CPO:

1. One shouldn't arbitrarily assume that it
   makes sense to certify every vehicle. Market
   Days Supply and Price to Market offer good
   gauges on the hot spots where the cost of
   certification meets the perceived value in the
   eyes of consumers.

2. It's essential to brand CPO vehicles effectively in online merchandising to distinguish
   their value proposition. Belowski makes sure
   the main photos for certified vehicles carry
   the Toyota CPO logo, and his descriptions
   note the certification right up front.
   "You have to differentiate," he says. Overall,
   Belowski believes such branding helps draw
   customers to vehicles, but adds that the
   person-to-person rundown of the CPO benefits typically seals customers on the value of
   the program.

3. It's more challenging to market non-
   certified used vehicles against CPO units
   at franchised stores. "I have that problem
   with Honda," Belowski says. "I can sell one
   if I'm a price leader, but if I'm positioned at
   number five, that vehicle will be around a

An "As-Is" Option for Recon Work

Check out this menu approach for reconditioning work:

Do the used vehicle inspection, complete the RO and then offer customers the option of buying the unit with or without the work completed at the dealership.

Dealer John Schenden of Pro Chrysler Jeep, Denver, says he stumbled on the idea but finds it works.

He estimates about 20 incremental sales a month flow from the program—with most taking the "as-is" option.

Schenden separates these factory program units from other stock. Salespeople offer them up when they can't make another deal work. "We'll say, 'follow me, I've got an idea,'" Schenden says.

I think it's a brilliant stroke. Why not give the customer the option? At worst, the store misses some service revenue, but there's still a shot at F&I if the customer buys the vehicle without the recon work.

Perhaps most intriguing, though, is the credibility-building it offers by extending the choice and being transparent about reconditioning costs.

Some say the idea's ripe for come-back trouble. Schenden says the program's been fine so far—in part, I suspect, because the deals firmly place responsibility for any problems with the customer.

"We've found a segment of the market that we were missing," he says. I think he's on to something.

while." (It should be noted that this certified vs. non-certified dynamic plays out more pointedly for CPO programs under brands with strong customer loyalty, such as Toyota, Mercedes, BMW, and Honda.)

PAINT PROCESS PROFICIENCY IS NOT ENOUGH

As much as I'd like to say that addressing the paint-based pressure points that occur when dealers and used vehicle managers adopt velocity-based metrics and management processes is all it takes for used vehicle success, I cannot.

The fact is, there's a whole separate degree of proficiency that's required in today's more efficient, volatile, and Internet-driven marketplace. This proficiency lies in what's become the pixel side of our business.

In today's marketplace, the vast majority of used vehicle customers begin their shopping process online, typically through online listing sites like *AutoTrader.com* and *Cars.com*. They also scout individual dealer websites, and check out online car shopping portals like *KBB.com*.

The upshot: If a dealer or a used vehicle manager neglects the pixel side of the business, they might as well keep the lights off and doors locked at their stores. Success in this Internet-driven retail environment requires the know-how to manage and massage online merchandising with the same care and attention many traditional dealers and used vehicle managers apply to their physical front line.

The next chapter details what this new breed of pixel proficiency is all about. It will also disclose and dissect what I believe are the critical, velocity-based pixel metrics that are essential for today's used vehicle success.

A SINFUL "PIXEL" PROBLEM

There's a disturbing disconnect—call it a sin even—
that exists at most dealerships.

While the Internet is undoubtedly the single most
important way of connecting dealerships with their
potential customers, few have much, if any, knowledge of how well they leverage this medium to
drive sales.

To be sure, many dealers and used vehicle managers know their inventories get posted to sites like
AutoTrader.com and *Cars.com*. Some will also have
a sense of how well these sites are working for their
stores.

Dealer/used vehicle manager: "I'm paying way too much money to my third-party site for the results I'm getting. We're spending $4,000 a month to sell only a half-dozen vehicles. That's nearly $700 a car. We're thinking of firing them."

Me: "Hold on a minute. Let me ask a couple questions before you do anything rash. How many Search Results Pages are you seeing on a monthly basis (SRPs)?"

Dealer/used vehicle manager: "I don't know."

But that's about as deep as the knowledge typically goes.

I say this based on the hundreds of conversations I've had in the past year or two with dealers and used vehicle managers about what I call the pixel side of our business—the online merchandising that's necessary in today's Internet-driven used vehicle marketplace to get on a customer's shopping list for a specific vehicle.

It's not uncommon for these conversations to follow this track:

Dealer/used vehicle manager: "I'm paying way too much money to my third-party site for the results I'm getting. We're spending $4,000 a month to sell only a half-dozen vehicles. That's nearly $700 a car. We're thinking of firing them."

Me: "Hold on a minute. Let me ask a couple questions before you do anything rash. How many Search Results Pages are you seeing on a monthly basis (SRPs)[10] ?"

---

[10]The Search Results Page metric is from *AutoTrader.com*, which I'm using solely for the sake of the example. *Cars.com*,

Dealer/used vehicle manager: "I don't know."

Me: "OK. How about your detailed page views (VDPs)?"

Dealer/used vehicle manager: "I don't know that either."

Me: "OK. I'm asking about these metrics because they provide insight into what might be happening with potential customers on the third-party site. Let's try something different. Go to the vendor's site and plug in a vehicle you've got for sale. How about that '07 Toyota Camry?"

Dealer/used vehicle manager: "Hang on. OK. I'm in. I'm typing in '07 Camry."

Me: "Great. Now, when the results show up, they'll be from highest to lowest price. Most customers will probably re-sort the listings to see the lowest price, so do the re-sort and tell me where your vehicle shows up."

Dealer/used vehicle manager: "Got it. Hmmm...I'm not seeing my car on the first page, or the second. Hang on. Let me check

---

Carsdirect, and other third-party classified sites offer similar benchmarks with different names to show dealers and used vehicle managers how online shoppers interact with their inventory listings.

a couple more. Oh, there it is. It's on the eighth page."

Me: "I see. How many total pages of '07 Camrys are there?"

Dealer/used vehicle manager: "Uhhh, 10 total pages."

Me: "OK. You're on the eighth page and it took you a couple of minutes to find it. Do you think a customer is likely to find your vehicle?"

Dealer/used vehicle manager: "Probably not."

Me: "What this tells me right away is that your price is near the top of the pack. That may or may not be OK. It depends on the vehicle. But it's fair to say the positioning isn't helping you connect with customers. The eighth page probably isn't in most customers' shopping sweet spot. How many photos are there, compared to the next vehicle?

Dealer/used vehicle manager: "Let's see... mine has 9, the next one has 27 and a video."

Me: "That may be another reason customers aren't clicking on your vehicle first. It's not

*as compelling. By the way, have you ever
done this exercise before?"*

Dealer/used vehicle manager: "No."

To me this kind of exchange is disturbing. How is it
that any dealer or used vehicle manager who claims
to be in the used vehicle business does not know
the fundamentals of the online game?

Yet these conversations are all too frequent and
familiar, and they suggest that many dealers and
used vehicle managers have a boatload of catching
up to do.

Automotive Internet retailing experts like Jared
Hamilton of *DrivingSales.com* agree that many
dealers misunderstand the role the Internet plays in
the marketing and merchandising of their vehicles.
To him, the third-party sites like *AutoTrader.com*
and *Cars.com* are the point-of-entry for most stores.

Hamilton also agrees that many dealers and used
vehicle managers "have a pile of data and don't
realize the gold it contains."

I like Hamilton's explanation for why this disconnect occurs. As a third-generation dealer, he
recognizes that stores often use imperfect systems
to count showroom traffic.

"I talk to my dad and he is super-lucky if he has
a good grasp on how many walk-ins, demos, and

write-ups the store gets," he says. "You're counting on an imperfect system to collect data, hoping it can it can give you accurate data. With the Internet, it's almost unfathomable that we can have this kind of really articulated data. It's like we've been trained not to look for it."

Hamilton's take is spot-on. At most stores, the dealer and used vehicle manager know, in a heartbeat, what their average foot traffic should look like on any given day of the week. They'd probably also know the traffic averages on a monthly basis, too. That's true for almost every dealer and used vehicle manager I've ever encountered. Foot traffic is a key barometer/predictor of sales; hence dealers and used vehicle managers pay attention to it, as they should.

But there's little attention to the metrics like Search Results Pages and Detailed Page Views –the equivalent of online drive-by and foot traffic—at most stores.

Dealers and used vehicle managers are too often like the ones in my hypothetical conversation. They simply aren't aware of the essential building blocks of what makes a solid-performing pixel strategy.

In addition, I've found there's very little attention paid to the kind of online presentation tactics that truly resonate with today's online consumers, including pictures, consistent pricing, videos, descriptions, and the like.

So the time has come for dealers and used vehicle managers to shed the pixel sins of the past and gain a better understanding of pixel proficiency and how to leverage it effectively for their used vehicle operations.

The knee-jerk reaction of many dealers and used vehicle managers when they're dissatisfied with the expense and results of their online merchandising vendors is to blame them for the perceived shortcomings.

The ultimate responsibility for understanding the fundamentals of online merchandising and pixel proficiency rests squarely on the shoulders of dealers and used vehicle managers who are generally unaware.

I am hopeful that our discussion here will spur more conversations and to-do action lists at stores across the country as dealers and used vehicle managers recognize what they should be doing to enhance their own online merchandising.

But this discussion is only the proverbial tip of the iceberg. The next chapters will further emphasize why I believe pixels are just as important as paint for success in today's Internet-driven used vehicle marketplace.

WHY "PIXEL PROFICIENCY" IS CRITICAL

Flashback: Remember the initial discussions sur-
rounding the impact the Internet would have on car
dealerships?

Along with it came predictions and concerns such
as those listed below:

- Factories would sell vehicles directly to consumers (a perception that execs like Jacque
  Nasser at Ford only helped fuel);

- Emotional debates about posting vehicle prices
  and inventories online;

- Scrambles to be the "exclusive first" to sign up for the hottest new lead generation provider;

- Scads of factory and third-party "build your website" options;

- Bitter disputes between Internet and showroom salespeople over who qualifies to be an Internet customer and who gets paid for those deals;

- Scores of Internet consultants who would turn dealerships into Internet stores;

- Fears of the demise of automotive retailing.

Thankfully, the "sky is falling" mentality has settled down. It's fair to say most dealers and used vehicle managers understand that the Internet plays such an essential role in today's business that they need to be online to have a shot at selling used vehicles.

The challenge now, however, is that just being online isn't good enough, particularly in used vehicles. This is true for several reasons:

1. Factories don't provide the same degree of online help for used vehicle departments as they do for new vehicle departments. Indeed, there are factory-sponsored online marketing and lead generation programs to support certified pre-owned programs, but beyond

that? Dealers and used vehicle managers are largely on their own when it comes to pixel support for their used vehicles.

2. Online customers are increasingly smarter about finding the sites they need to aid their shopping and product comparisons. Research from the Pew Internet and American Life Projects show that 80 percent of U.S. households have an Internet connection and they aren't just checking email.[11]

   The upshot: Consumers know a good online experience when they encounter one. They know how to navigate websites to find what they need and they get annoyed when an online process is cumbersome or deliberately obtuse.

3. More dealerships are getting smarter about finding, targeting, and selling to today's online used vehicle buyers. These dealers and used vehicle managers know their SRPs and VDPs. They've nailed down processes to post pictures quickly, write compelling vehicle descriptions, price vehicles competitively and provide a customer-centric experience.

   Some of these same stores are also heavily into advanced pixel proficiency that involves

---

[11] Pew Internet and American Life Project, http://www.pewinternet.org/Trend-Data/Online-Activities-20002009.aspx.

online marketing campaigns, search engine optimization (SEO), search engine marketing (SEM), social media engagement, and other outreach intended to enhance their store brands and sell more customers.

Among the stores that focus on search-related marketing, those who strike first will have a long-standing advantage. Search engines give credit to the longevity of web-sites and the traffic they capture—a factor that means "first to market is everything," notes Brian Benstock, the velocity and pixel-savvy GM and Vice President for Queens, N.Y.-based Paragon Honda.

This should inject some degree of urgency into ratcheting up the pixel proficiency at dealerships, particularly those where dealers and used vehicle managers still rely on traditional paint-based ways of managing their used vehicle operations and have yet to fully leverage their presence on third-party sites like *AutoTrader.com* and *Cars.com*.

4. Pixel proficiency is a key stage toward a successful, velocity-based approach to managing used vehicle operations. It's one thing for a store to get all of its paint-based metrics—Market Days Supply, Price to Market and Cost to Market—in line with the market. It's quite another when a dealership

takes that foundation and builds upon it an efficient, velocity-minded online marketing and merchandising platform that positions inventory in places and at price points consumers will find appealing.

THE BUILDING BLOCKS OF "PIXEL PROFICIENCY"

I've been tracking the pixel proficiency of a composite of over 100 velocity-minded dealerships to gain a better understanding of what matters most when it comes to the online merchandising of used vehicles.

From a broad perspective, the dynamics around the placement, pricing, and positioning of used vehicle inventory can be divided into two main buckets— how consumers shop for used vehicles online and how dealerships can best capture the interests of online used vehicle shoppers.

Bucket 1: How consumers shop for used vehicles online and what they see. Industry statistics suggest that the majority of used vehicle shoppers like to see comparisons of vehicles when they shop. This explains the popularity of sites such as *AutoTrader.com, Cars.com, KBB.com,* and others. In a study conducted in late 2008, J.D. Power and Associates affirms these sites are the dominant players for online used vehicle shoppers and notes that shoppers are spending an increasing amount of time (about nine hours on average) researching, reviewing, and comparing vehicles they might purchase.[12]

"Consumers are going deeper in their searches," affirms Mitch Golub. "They're looking at more vehicles."

Consumers typically start their shopping queries at search engines, but the online listing sites offer the best unit-to-unit comparison functionality. In addition, these sites spend lots of money on advertising to brand themselves as go-to destinations for consumers.

And what about dealers' own websites? The importance of these sites should not be underestimated. But, for the most part, these sites currently play a secondary role to third-party sites when it comes to used vehicle shoppers. This dynamic is changing a bit but for our discussion of pixel proficiency, I'm going to limit the focus to the external sites that a) are utilized by a wider array of used vehicle shoppers with regularity and frequency and b) represent the best initial investment of time, money, and attention for dealers and used vehicle managers who seek to enhance their pixel proficiency.

---

[12]J.D. Power & Associates 2008 Used Vehicle Market Report, Dec. 2008, http://www.jdpower.com/corporate/news/releases/pressrelease.aspx?ID=2008267

These third-party sites typically break into two camps:

1. **Information-oriented sites, such as** *KBB.com,* **that provide a wealth of resources and car-buying pointers for consumers, as well as links to inventory listings.** From these listings, sites like *KBB.com* sell leads to dealers and used vehicle managers. Comparatively speaking, the leads these sites generate are less vehicle-specific than emails, queries, and calls that result from used vehicle shoppers landing on a dealer's used vehicle listings from sites like *AutoTrader.com* and *Cars. com.*

2. **Online classified sites.** These are the *Auto-Trader.com* and *Cars.com* sites that host dealers' inventories and allow consumers the ability to search and sort listings in a variety of ways (by price, year/make/model, zip codes). These sites, which are really the online equivalent of the newspaper classified ads that dealerships purchased to advertise used vehicles in the past, typically do not let consumers drill into specific features and equipment in the initial search stages. Instead, online buyers narrow their choices and must-have options the deeper they explore inventory listings.

There are some important fundamental considerations dealers and used vehicle managers should
understand about these third-party sites:

Pay-to-play nature: Dealers can list their inventories for free on these sites, but they have
monetized the e-real estate in a way that pushes
dealerships to spend more money to achieve
maximum presence and merchandising flexibility. This is not necessarily a bad thing but
the lack of in-depth knowledge I've discerned at
most traditional dealerships suggests that some
dealers and used vehicle managers are paying
for functionality and e-real estate they're not
using as effectively as they could or should.

Size matters: Few dealers and used vehicle
managers understand that while sites like *Auto-
Trader.com* and *Cars.com* are ubiquitous, they
don't carry the same weight and potential for
every store. This occurs for two reasons:

1. The number of active shoppers varies from
    market to market. I've seen velocity dealer-
    ships in my 100-store sample with active
    shopper tallies that range from 25,000 to
    400,000 and above. The average active
    shopper tally in my sample on one of these
    third-party sites is 120,000. Most dealers
    and used vehicle managers are unaware of
    the active shopper statistic for their respec-

tive markets—a foundational data point for pixel proficiency and for evaluating why one site may work better than another.

It's absolutely true that many dealers and used vehicle managers have a sense that one site works better for them than another. But when I hear this comment and drill down, I rarely hear anyone mention active shopper stats to draw this conclusion.

2. The number of inventory listings, and their relevance to a given market, play a key role in capturing a consumer's eye online. In my 100-store sample, there's no question that velocity dealers with 200 units listed online get more SRPs and VDPs than dealers with only 40 units. This is true even when both stores have properly aligned their inventories to the Market Days Supply metric to assure they have the most in-demand vehicles.

As consumers are exploring these initial search listings pages, and then clicking to see a specific vehicle, they like to view photos, videos, and other features. This is also where price sensitivity and preference for one dealer's vehicle versus another's comes into play. It is also the point, for some consumers, where their online shopping stops.

Here's what I mean: Assume that two vehicles from competing dealers are comparable, they are both priced competitively, and they both tout the features and value that resonate with a buyer. This consumer might call or email the stores. He/she might also print out a map or print a copy of the individual vehicle listings.

The third-party sites track these behaviors and they can be useful drill-downs to show the degree to which consumers are interacting with a dealership's inventory listings. But the usefulness of this data only goes so far.

This is because an estimated 60 percent (some velocity dealers and used vehicle managers think it might be as high as 85 percent) of the shoppers who visit these sites will never call or email the store they intend to visit. They just show up. And when they do, they expect to find the vehicle they spotted available at the online advertised price. This dynamic speaks to a comment noted in the prior chapter that customers who call a dealership are ready to buy. So are many of the customers that just show up.

"You can't just be looking at emails and phone calls," says Chip Perry at *AutoTrader.com*. He notes an *AutoTrader.com*/Northwood University study from early 2009 that reports 60 percent of online shoppers do not raise their hands prior to visiting a dealership[13]. "Stores that only focus on chasing

---

[13] http://autotrader.mediaroom.com/index.php?s=43&item =148

leads are likely missing 60 percent of the closing opportunities."

Perry suggests this propensity for online shoppers to just show up signals a need for traditional dealerships to ensure their show-room sales team understands they are often dealing with well-informed customers. He recommends initial upfront qualifiers that identify these shoppers and respect what they likely already know about a vehicle and its price.

"Dealers need to take off their dealer glasses and put on their consumer glasses," Perry adds. When they do, they'll likely arrive at showroom sales processes that are bet-ter suited to work effectively with today's Internet-enabled buyers.

> *"Dealers need to take off their dealer glasses and put on their consumer glasses," Perry adds. When they do, they'll likely arrive at showroom sales processes that are better suited to work effectively with today's Internet-enabled buyers.*

Bucket 2: How dealerships can best capture online shopper interest. One of the blessings of the third-party sites is that they are structured in a way that enables dealers and used vehicle managers to zero in on what mat-ters most to capture customers. That is, each of the sites has specific elements that dealerships can leverage and light up to showcase their vehicle listings, depending on how much they decide to pay.

In essence, they are aiming to capture online shoppers' pick and click behaviors that occur when third-party sites serve up vehicle listings for consumers to review.

For example, when the sites list the equivalent of a Search Result Page that shows a series of vehicles from the sorts customers choose, they only see a top-line view: A photo, a brief description, and a few clues about what's in store for them if they click on the listing. Let's call this the bait for buyers.

From my 100-store sample, the velocity-minded dealerships that are more effective at baiting their top-line listings see more action than those that don't. This means playing up vehicle descriptions and having ample photos and video. For example, it seems more likely that a consumer would pick and click on a top-line listing that baits them with 27 photos and video, versus one that offers only nine photos and no video.

Perry agrees with this conclusion and notes that many dealers and used vehicle managers still take shortcuts on these important elements.

Of course, there are a myriad of variables that affect these consumer pick and click behaviors: the quality of photos/videos, the degree to which descriptions are compelling, the price of a vehicle, the unit itself, the premium placements dealerships might purchase, and more.

As Bill Pearson says, "you've got to do them all well, because they all play a part."

Other factors that affect the ability of dealers and used vehicle managers to capture online shopper interest are:

Inventory the market craves. I mentioned earlier that size matters in terms of inventory quantities dealerships post on third-party sites. More inventory means more chances for online consumers to review a store's inventory and follow the pick and click behaviors.

But it's more than just adding more vehicles to a store's inventory listings. The vehicles need to reflect the high-demand, low-supply characteristics measured by the Market Days Supply metric. The vehicles need to be right for a market, something traditional dealers and used vehicle managers with franchise first and gut-based biases will often miss.

Think of it this way: If a store stocked 1,000 Yugos and posted them online, would it see much consumer interest?

The answer is obviously no. But it's a hypothetical question that underscores how imperative it is to stock in-demand vehicles that the market deems worthy of the investment.

I would guess that many of the dealers and used vehicle managers who have beaten up their third-party site reps over poor results may not have recognized the role their own inventory mix played in driving outcomes that did not meet expectations.

Consistent, market-based prices. This is where velocity-minded dealers who use metrics like Price to Market have an edge on their traditional counterparts. Consumers are price-sensitive, and they understand when a dealer's asking price reflects the market. Likewise, they can spot when a vehicle's priced too high for a market.

This does not mean that every dealer and used vehicle manager needs to have the lowest price to attract shoppers—but it certainly doesn't hurt. Velocity dealers and used vehicle managers know that if they set a vehicle to be a price leader in its segment compared to other competing vehicles, they will see spikes in consumer interest. This is a valuable insight that helps them move out aging inventory to make way for fresher units with greater profit potential.

Mitch Golub says he's seeing a sizable increase in the number of dealers in the past year who are actively making price changes on their vehicles. "It's increased precipitously," he says. "The best-performing dealers are those who are changing prices as much as four to five times a day."

This sensitivity to price reflects the fact that a wider number of dealers and used vehicle managers recognize that price is important and competitive prices are paramount.

Golub and I share a laugh when we discuss pricing and how it has come full circle from the early days of the Internet when dealers and used vehicle managers resisted showing any prices at all online. As it happens, the fears that consumers would take posted prices and beat up salespeople on every deal have been replaced with the reality that consumers expect to see prices online and, if they don't, quite often move past the un-priced vehicle to shop vehicles that show a price.

A cautionary point about pricing: It's not uncommon for consumers, after they review a dealership's vehicle listing on a third-party site, to check out the store's website to confirm that a vehicle is available and to find out more about how the store conducts business.

This is a critical part of the shopping funnel that creates a few challenges for dealers and used vehicle managers:

1. **Pricing parity:** Between the third-party sites and dealers' own websites, there are often

multiple back-end feeds that handle the
updates of prices, photos, and other bait
elements to individual vehicle listings. It's
not uncommon for snags to occur that result
in the same vehicle being priced differently
across these multiple platforms. Consumers can spot these inconsistencies, and they
are potential interest-killers as it suggests a
dealership is less transparent about pricing
than others. It suggests old school pricing
and sales practices that can be a turn-off for
today's buyers.

The good news: Today's technology allows
audits of pricing across the third-party
platforms and dealer websites to ensure customers see the consistency they seek when
they shop online.

2. **Showroom parity.** At some velocity dealerships, dealers and used vehicle managers
capitalize on the fact that they're using the
Price to Market metric to set their used
vehicle prices. They tell consumers they
mine the Internet for prices, and set theirs
accordingly.

At Sam Swope Auto Group in Louisville,
Kentucky, they call this Internet Value Pric-
ing. "We address this right up front," says
Cary Donovan. "We'll even go online and
say, 'Let's make sure this is the correct price.'"
The approach builds credibility with custom-

ers and eases anxiety they might have had about the store sticking to the price they saw online.

Donovan adds that it's not uncommon, given the dealer group's daily attention to the Price to Market metric, for customers to get an even lower price than the one that they saw online. "We go with the price that's posted on a given day—which is often more favorable for customers," he says.

Peek Into the Murky Water

% of vehicles in the shop for more than 72 business hours?

% of vehicles on your lot that don't have a window sticker matching current price?

% of vehicles that have multiple prices?

% of vehicles with unacceptable time to Internet?

% of vehicles on your physical lot not yet on the Internet?

% of vehicles with no online price?

% of vehicles with incorrect prices?

% of vehicles that are not being published to all designated sites?

"PIXEL PROFICIENCY" PITFALLS

There are a lot of spots along the path to pixel proficiency where things can run amuck.

One of the key trouble spots is properly allocating the work that's necessary to be effective with online merchandising and marketing.

At many stores, these responsibilities often fall to the used vehicle managers. In some cases, this translates to a savvy paint-minded manager being charged with pixel proficiency when he or she lacks the time and/or skills to do so effectively.

The upshot: It's unreasonable to expect any one person, particularly those who have long been paint-minded experts, to do this job. It takes a coordinated effort across a dealership organization to effectively execute a winning pixel strategy for today's used vehicle marketplace.

A second pitfall results from the distrust and disinterest many dealers and used vehicle managers hold toward the third-party site reps that make monthly visits to their stores.

This pitfall became crystal-clear to me during a recent lunch when I was discussing the relationships two dealers had with their third-party reps.

Dealer #1: "I can't stand my rep. Every time he's here, he's always asking me to spend more money. I don't even make time for him anymore. I let my used vehicle manager handle that."

Dealer #2: "That's a big mistake, Don. You need to hug that guy. You need to love the guy you hate. You spend a lot of money with them and they hold the key to a lot of information that you need to excel."

This disparity is both striking and profound. It certainly explains why some dealers and used vehicle managers lack any real understanding of SRPs and VDPs or their equivalents and other fundamentals that drive success on third-party sites.

From my conversations with *Cars.com* and *AutoTrader.com*, the view of Dealer #2 is gaining ground. "We're seeing higher-level people in dealerships showing up at our training," says Golub at *Cars.com*.

AutoTrader.com's Chip Perry notes that the company is investing heavily in training its reps to play a more active, consulting role with their dealership clients to help them gain a better understanding of the existing metrics to improve their pixel proficiency.

"PIXEL PROFICIENCY" 101 : NEW BENCHMARKS TO GUIDE SUCCESS

It's impossible for anyone to perform at their best if they lack an understanding of what defines best.

In business, achievement or success is often defined by clear benchmarks and goals. In used vehicles, our historic benchmarks have been gross profit per vehicle retailed (PVR) and sales volumes.

It should be clear from this book that these metrics remain useful in today's more efficient and volatile used vehicle marketplace, but they are crude barometers compared to the more market-attuned and data-rich management insights that come from guiding used vehicle operations with paint-based metrics such as Market Days Supply, Price to Market, and Cost to Market.

When it comes to online merchandising of used vehicles, or pixel proficiency, our industry has not yet clearly defined the benchmarks that offer a clear path for where time and effort should be focused to most efficiently and effectively drive success.

In the previous chapter, we noted how dealers and used vehicle managers often fail to pay attention to the basic metrics that flow from the third-party vendors that provide the shopping portals most used vehicle buyers pass through as they shop for the car that's right for them.

But even with these metrics, such as Search Results Pages (SRPs) and Vehicle Detail Pages (VDPs) and their equivalents, there's little understanding of what constitutes a good job. For example, 25,000 search results pages or 10,000 detailed page views sound like big numbers, but what do they mean? Should these numbers be 200,000 and 12,000, respectively? What kind of conversion ratio might dealers and used vehicle managers expect from their SRPs? What is the relationship between these metrics and sales?

From my study of 100 velocity dealerships, I've come up with benchmarks to help dealers and used vehicle managers gain a clearer understanding of the baseline performance they should expect from their efforts to merchandise and sell used vehicles online.

These benchmarks offer insights to help dealers and managers enhance their pixel proficiency. The benchmarks offer clues on any hiccups that might occur in the shopping funnel. For example, if a store has a high number of SRPs, and few VDPs, it suggests something's wrong with the initial bait that's meant to entice a click-through, or it may signal a problem with pricing.

Similarly, if a store has a low number of SRPs and a high conversion rate to VDPs, it suggests the bait is working fine but something is off in the initial positioning, quantity of inventory, pricing, or vehicle mix.

It's my hope that the pixel benchmarks I've developed from my 100-store sample will help answer these important questions. The ultimate goal for dealers and managers is to become more astute about their pixel proficiency and enjoy the rewards of the additional used vehicle sales volumes and profits that await those who properly leverage this proficiency.

Before sharing these new benchmarks, however, I'd like to address a few problems with the benchmarks many dealers and used vehicle managers currently use to evaluate ROI from third-party listing sites and demonstrate why the new pixel benchmarks offer a better way forward.

Problems With "Pick and Click" Benchmarks

Before reading this next section, I might suggest that dealers and used vehicle managers remove any untethered items from their immediate reach. What I'm about to share may raise the blood pressure for some readers.

In my discussions with dealers and used vehicle managers about the ROI they get from third-party sites, and the often-reflexive dissatisfaction with results, I've come to realize that these ROI benchmarks are flawed.

These benchmarks are typically the cost-per-lead and cost-per-vehicle sold. Each of these flows from the pick and click behaviors that result when consumers drill down to a specific vehicle listing (a VDP or its equivalent).

That is, once an online shopper takes an interest in a vehicle, he/she may make a phone call, send an email, or print out directions to a store or the vehicle listing itself.

Let's examine both of these calculations and why they don't show a true picture of the two-way nature of a third-party site's performance for a dealership:

Cost per lead. For this benchmark, dealers and used vehicle managers take the number of phone calls or emails they receive from a third-party site, and divide that figure into the total cost they pay on a monthly basis for the site's listing services.

So if a dealership receives 100 phone calls from a third-party site, and pays $5,000 a month to list its inventory, the cost per lead is $50. Most dealers and used vehicle managers believe that this is an accurate read on the traction they receive from the third-party site and the effectiveness of the site's ability to draw in customers.

I believe this calculation is problematic. For example:

Reason 1: The 100 phone calls represent only a portion of the customers who viewed the inventory. Remember the *AutoTrader. com*/Northwood University data I referenced earlier? For every 100 shoppers who visit and view used vehicle listings, an estimated 60 percent will show up at a store without making a call or sending an email.

By some estimates, phone calls and leads represent hand-raisers who account for about 20 percent of all the shoppers who may view a dealership's inventory listings. So, the cost per lead calculation is only counting a portion of the site's ability to attract customers.

> **Reason 2:** Most dealers and used vehicle managers understand that the costs for individual third-party sites vary. *AutoTrader. com*, for example, offers more advertising options and functionality for dealers and used vehicle managers who sign up and pay for their Partner and Alpha programs.

By definition, the leads that flow from this site will cost more than others. So a strict, cost-per-lead analysis would suggest *AutoTrader. com* may not be worth the money compared to another vendor.

This is a misguided conclusion. In addition to not accounting for *all* of the shoppers who may become customers via a third-party site, the cost-per-lead calculation doesn't capture the value that leads from one site might offer compared to another. What if the phone calls from one third-party site resulted in more F&I income? What if one site proves to be a better outlet for price leaders, high-line vehicles, and/or early model vehicles?

The cost-per-lead calculation does not capture these nuances. A store that strictly follows cost-per-lead calculations to determine ROI could be missing out on some key opportunities.

> **Reason 3:** The simple cost-per-lead calculation fails to account for other critical details, such as the number of unique vehicles receiving leads. For example, what if 20 of the 100 monthly leads came from a single vehicle? While it's true that a lead is a lead, this additional information might affect the way the dealership values these leads and assesses their online listing costs.

> **Reason 4:** What if a dealership's own listings lack the quality and depth of photos, descriptions, and value proposition on its vehicles compared to competitors? How does a cost-per-lead calculation account for these pixel deficiencies? Is it fair to hold a third-party site accountable for a store's own pixel execution shortcomings?

My point here is that the cost-per-lead calculation has value, but it does not definitively offer any make-or-break ROI conclusions about a third-party site's performance nor does it deliver any solid, practical insight on how to fix shortcomings in a store's online merchandising and pixel presentation.

Cost-Per-Vehicle Sold: This calculation, which divides the monthly cost for a third-party site by the number of vehicles a store gives it credit for delivering, falls victim to some of the same shortcomings that render the cost-per-lead calculations ineffective as a barometer of a third-party site's performance.

In addition to the fact that this calculation does not account for online shoppers who visit a site and view listings but do not call or email before showing up at a dealership, the cost-per-vehicle sold calculation incorrectly saddles the third-party vendor with accountability for a store's sales processes.

For example, let's say the store in our example above that spent $5,000 a month sells 20 vehicles from the 100 calls it received from its third-party partner (a 20 percent conversion rate). That translates to a cost-per-vehicle sold of $250.

The problem? The third-party site has nothing to do with the ability of a store to convert leads into sold customers. What if the store was able to close 35 percent of the 100 leads it received? If it did, that would put the cost-per-vehicle at $143. In this instance, dealers and used vehicle managers would likely view that as a positive, and credit themselves for a high close ratio. I doubt they'd turn to their third-party vendor and say, "You did a great job helping us close our leads."

Likewise, the cost-per-vehicle sold metric also fails to account for a dealership's own shortcomings with its online merchandising and pixel presentation. It does not assess how many customers got away because they didn't like what they saw on the detailed vehicle listing.

Now, I suspect some readers are poking holes in my assessment of the value of these pick and click-based ROI calculations.

The most obvious hole might come from dealers and used vehicle managers who have great faith in their showroom traffic assessment tools that capture and detail how an "up" arrived at their stores.

These dealers and used vehicle managers will say their salespeople and BDC teams are well trained and know how to properly and respectfully ask customers to detail the specific third-party sites they visited and where they saw the vehicle that brought them to the store.

To them, I tip my hat. They have apparently solved one of the most persistent and problematic issues that have plagued dealerships from the beginning of time. In addition, they must have figured out a way to ensure that every customer remembers their online shopping and shares it truthfully.

Most dealerships lack the kind of traffic-tracking sophistication that would make the cost-per-lead and cost-per-sale metrics truly reliable gauges of a third-party site's performance. For them I would suggest that new pixel metrics are more reliable ways to assess the blend of the third-party site's platform and a dealership's ability to effectively execute its pixel proficiency within the platform.

As the old saying goes, "it takes two to tango," and this is especially true with the third-party sites.

NEW BENCHMARKS TO GAUGE PIXEL PROFICIENCY

As noted earlier, dealers and used vehicle managers need to better understand the equivalent of SRPs and VDPs, and how they relate to each other, to get the best read possible on their pixel proficiency on third-party sites.

It's through understanding these data points and related benchmarks that dealers and used vehicle managers can begin to see where they may be falling short with their online merchandising and pixel presentation of used vehicles.

The new benchmark metrics I'm about to share flow from my study of 100 velocity-minded dealerships across the country. Each of these stores retails at least 100 used vehicles a month, they hail from markets of different sizes, and their respective inventories possess similar paint metric characteristics—Market Days Supply, Price to Market and Cost to Market.

This pool was selected to normalize the study: By meeting the benchmark averages for the paint metrics, these stores all carry inventory their markets crave at price points that are compelling to potential buyers. This normalization is necessary because, as noted in the last chapter, the type of inventory and prices for specific units play a key role in whether an online shopper will click on a dealership's vehicle listing or go to another one.

So with this normalization, we can begin to examine the relationships between SRPs and VDPs or their equivalents.

A quick refresher: SRPs are merely opportunities. The statistic represents the number of times online shoppers viewed a search results page that included a specific dealership's inventory listing. VDPs represent the next, more valuable step: The number of consumers who actually clicked on a dealership's inventory listing to more closely examine a vehicle.

So, given the interplay between SRPs and VDPs, here are the baseline benchmarks that matter most:

SRP Baseline Benchmark: On average, the velocity-minded stores in the sample group generate 250,000 SRPs each month. Some see as many as 1.5 million, some as few as 25,000. The best I can tell, the difference owes mostly to three factors:

1. The number of active shoppers in a dealer's market area. The dealership that sees 1.5 million often has a larger shopper base than the store with 25,000 SRPs.

2. The amount and position of screen real estate the velocity dealerships leverage on the third-party sites. The dealer that buys up every advertising option available has positioned himself to realize a higher number of SRPs than a dealer that has a more limited investment. It is an inescapable fact that screen real estate matters a lot in getting your vehicles noticed. Dealers often balk at online sales reps that propose additional expenditures while the truth is these incremental investments pale in comparison to the price of purchasing less effective conventional media such as newspaper, radio, or television.

3. The size of each dealer's inventory. The dealer with higher SRPs has 400 units in inventory, while the second dealer carries about 50 units.

Now here's where this example gets interesting: The second dealer decided he wanted to increase sales volumes. He bought up all the advertising options available on the third-party site and increased his inventory. His SRP count now runs nearly 400,000. It's still less than the dealer with 1.5 million SRPs, but the example shows that inventory size and screen real estate are critical drivers for SRP counts.

> **VDP Conversion Benchmark:** Given the vari-
> ability in market size noted in the above SRP
> discussion, the number of VDPs is less impor-
> tant for benchmark purposes than the ratio
> of conversions from SRPs to VDPs. From my
> study, dealers and used vehicle managers should
> aim for a conversion rate benchmark of 3 to 4
> percent to be considered pixel proficient. So, if
> a store has 100,000 SRPs, they should expect a
> minimum of 3,000 VDPs.

If the VDP conversion rate is lower, it suggests a problem with the pixel bait that appears with a vehicle listing on a search result page: Is there a photo? Does it look good? Is the price correct? Is the description fresh and snappy? Or does its VIN decode text read like Ben Stein's monotone: "Bueller...Bueller?[14]"

Likewise, if the VDP tally is higher, it suggests a store understands the SRP sweet spots that entice customers to click deeper.

In my study, velocity stores that consistently hit this conversion ratio each month sustained their sales

---

[14] http://en.wikipedia.org/wiki/Ferris_Bueller%27s_Day_Off

volumes while stores that fell below the ratio did
not. It's worth noting that when the ratio dropped,
the dealers and used vehicle managers report some
aspect of their pixel processes fell short.

For example, the dealer who bought up all the
advertising options to increase his SRP tally saw
an unexpected two-point drop in his VDP conversions. The dip caused him to look harder at his
pixel presentation and processes. His conclusion:
The additional volume was not being well managed—photos and prices were missing online.
After correcting these errors, his VDP conversions
returned to a pixel proficient level. It should therefore be noted that it is not prudent to purchase
additional screen real estate and/or increase inventory size until and unless the dealership is able to
convert SVPs into VDPs efficiently. To do so would
be the equivalent of spending additional money
to drive more traffic to the showroom without
adequate sales personnel to handle the incremental
"ups."

Such is the nature of pixel proficiency. It takes a
mix of investment and trial and error to find the
sweet spot of inventory mix, pixel bait, and price
to consistently connect with online shoppers. This
type of hands-on attention is critical for dealerships who aspire to do a better job with their used
vehicle operations.

Dealers and used vehicle managers who pay greater attention to SRP and VDP benchmarks, and understand the paint and pixel elements that drive them, will be better positioned to capture consumer attention and will see more opportunities to sell vehicles.

As noted earlier, the reps from third-party sites recognize that dealers and used vehicle managers need to develop a better understanding of what matters most to drive consumer interest in a store's used vehicle listings.

Here's a two-part agenda I would recommend every dealer and used vehicle manager follow for the next monthly visit from third-party site reps:

1. **A review of SRP and VDP benchmarks.** The discussion should address expectations, given the number of active shoppers in a market and comparable stats from competitors.

2. **Deeper discussions of any differences/variations in a store's pixel performance.** Prior to the meeting, dealers and used vehicle managers should do their own review to see what they think might be falling short—whether it's photos, price, inventory mix, descriptions, etc. These insights will drive a more fruitful and telling discussion with the third-party site reps.

Every dealer and used vehicle manager has heard the old management phrase: You have to inspect what you expect. The benchmarks in this chapter lay the groundwork for what dealerships should expect from their online listings on third-party sites. Now, the time has come for pixel inspections to begin in earnest.

A REAL-TIME AUDIT OF "PIXEL PROFICIENCY"

It's pretty telling what one sees by taking off the "dealer glasses" and putting on the "consumer glasses."

For a little fun, I decided to jump on the *Auto-Trader.com* website and do a couple vehicle searches. My thinking: Let's see how dealers in a 25-mile range of my Chicago-area zip code are doing with their "pixel proficiency." I settled on two different searches for vehicles, and opted to solely view the listings pages.

Here's what I found:

"Family Car" Search Stats

Total number of dealers: *(one independent)*	19
Number of dealers with multiple listings:	5
Total number of private sellers:	1
Average number of photos/listing:	16
Number of listings without photos:	1
Number of listings with 27 photos*:	3
Number of listings with videos: *(4 from two dealers, 2 from individual stores)*	6
Number of listings with Carfax reports:	8

*27 is the maximum number of photos AutoTrader.com allows.

Search 1: The "Family Car" Search. I figured I'd look for what might be a typical second car, and entered a broad query for a 2004-2009 four-door sedan, priced between $12,000 and $15,000. There were 25 pages of results, so I set a low to high price sort and looked closely at the vehicles on the first page.

The findings are eye-opening:

- **Inconsistencies across listings from the same stores and dealer groups.** Of the five stores that had multiple listings, four offered vehicles with different numbers of photos on each listed unit; one offered a video on one listing but not another.

- **Inconsistent descriptions and/ or pricing:** To me, a one-word change (One Owner! to 1 OWNER!), doesn't count as a compelling or unique vehicle description but this is how a Nissan store differentiated two '06 Nissan Altimas

(one blue, one gold). Another potential
problem: Despite the exact same equipment
and an 11,100-mile odometer difference, the
store listed both vehicles at $12,490. These
strike me as signs of an inattentive hand.

- **Varying degrees of snap in vehicle descriptions.**
  Of the three descriptions below, which one
  comes from the keyboard of the sole private
  seller on my listing page?

  *(A) Power Steering, Power Brakes, Power
  Door Locks, Power Windows, Alloy
  Wheels, Trip Odometer, Tachometer, Air
  Conditioning, Tilt Steering Wheel, Cruise
  Control, Interval Wipers, Rear Defroster,
  Console, Front Bucket Seats, Cloth
  Upholstery, Center Arm Rest, Drive*

  *(B) All scheduled maintenance, Always
  garaged, Fully loaded, Ice cold A/C,
  Looks & runs great, Must see, New
  tires, No accidents, Non-smoker, One
  owner, Power everything, Perfect first car,
  Runs & drives great, Satellite radio, Very
  clean...*

  *(C) *CONSTRUCTION SALE NOW IN
  PROGRESS******CALL NOW TO
  MAKE AN OFFER***, Tilt Wheel, Dual*

*Front Air Bags, Power Windows, Air
Conditioning, Power Door Locks, MP3
(Single CD), Power Steering, Cruise
Control, AM/FM Stereo, PWR FRONT
DISC/REAR DRUM BRAK.*

The answer: (B). There's no question the text reads
and feels better than the other two.

While we're on the subject of vehicle descriptions
and having a little fun, check out these descriptions
from the listing page and my commentary[15]:

From the "cluttered cliché" file: *This
searing-hot 2007 Chevrolet Impala is the
high-performance car you've been aching
to get your hands on. All good things must
come to an end, but don't worry...it'll
be there in your driveway next morning,
waiting for another adrenaline...*

My take: Did you drink too much Red Bull?

From the "kill 'em with ALL CAPS" file:
*LOADED LACROSSE HERE!! FUEL
EFFICIENT V6 ENGINE KEEPS THIS
LUXURY SEDAN GOING WITHOUT
KILLING YOU AT THE PUMP!! WHAT
LUXURY YOU ASK?? HOW ABOUT A
SUNROOF!! FULL POWER TILT AND*

---

[15]My apologies to anyone who recognizes a description here.
My aim is to educate, not humiliate. I hope you view the
feedback as valuable.

SLIDE!! COMFORTABLE LEATHER
SEATS ARE FULL POWER AND
HEATED!! AM/FM/CD

My take: Aside from the ALL CAPS, I like how
this description plays up fuel economy and
value-add features like a sunroof.

From the "honesty" file: *Stop by to*
Experience the (dealer name removed)
Difference !!! – This vehicle shows no sign
of paint work. This vehicle was tastefully
optioned. With just 38,946 miles, this car
is barely broken in. This vehicle has been
inspected. Very clean interior!

My take: Honesty is never a bad policy. I like
the language. But I wonder what happened to
the tasteful options? Did somebody steal them?

From the "folksy" file: *"THIS LIKE*
NEW GALANT IS PRICED TO SELL!
(NAME REMOVED) OUR USED CAR
MGR SAYS THERE'S OVER 42K MILES
OF FULL FACTORY WARRANTY
LEFT!! THIS GALANT QUALIFIES
FOR EXTRA LOW-LOW-LOW
PAYMENTS!!!YOU BETTER HURRY IN
AND GET THIS GREAT DEAL WHILE
IT S...

My take: Nice personal touch to include the manager's name. FYI: The "caps lock" key is located at the left of most computer keyboards, just above the "shift" key.

From the "Bueller Bueller" file: *Driver Air Bag, Passenger Air Bag, A/C, AM/FM Stereo, CD Player, Front Disc/Rear Drum Brakes, Rear Defrost, Child Safety Locks, Front Wheel Drive, Auto-On Headlights, Daytime Running Lights, Power Driver Mirror, Pass-Through Rear Seat, Cloth Seats.*

My take: Thank God! This car has rear drum brakes. I was looking for a set of those.

Search 2: The "Hot Seller" Search. My goal here was to see how listings might look for a hot-selling used vehicle. Would they showcase a greater degree of pixel proficiency, given the hot-model status?

I searched for a used 2005-2009 Prius entering the same zip code as for the Family Car Search above. I didn't set any price parameters, or specify a certified vehicle. I sorted by low-to-high price, and looked closely at the first 25 listings (see stats box, next page).

Again, the listings were revealing:

- **Consistent use of videos.** Three stores used videos consistently across their listings, though the number of photos they offered across listings varied by two or three photos.

- **Fewer "Bueller Bueller" descriptions.** By my count, 17 of the listings showed some sign of a human touch. Theme-wise, "Go Green" played prominently in descriptions from two dealerships, a wise nod to the hybrid's appeal.

- **Favoring photos/videos over descriptions.** One of the stores that offered a full complement of photos and video included the same vehicle description for three of its four units.

- **One "Alpha" dealer.** This dealer has invested additional money to have a logo/listing appear on *AutoTrader.com's* "search-in-progress" screen and a prominent listing on the listing page.

- **Expired financing options.** Vehicle descriptions from two separate dealers noted reduced-rate financing deals with expired "act now" dates.

"Hot Seller" Search Stats

Total number of dealers: *(no independent or non-Toyota dealers)*	11
Number of dealers with multiple listings:	6
Total number of private sellers:	0
Average number of photos/listing:	16
Number of listings without photos: *(all "newly listed")*	3
Number of listings with 27 photos:	7
Number of listings with videos: *(all from three dealers)*	10
# of listings with Carfax reports:	18

- **ALL CAPs continues.** Nine of the 25 listings
  were in ALL CAPs. I'm blind, so this doesn't
  really bother me. But I'm told with conviction
  from my wife, family, and colleagues that it's
  ANNOYING and it is considered shouting.
  That's enough for me to suggest dealers and
  used vehicle managers discontinue the practice.

All in all, it's safe to say that pixel proficiency
remains spotty across the results of my two random
searches. Some dealers and used vehicle managers
do a better job, others do a not-so-good job. The
fact that I found so many pixel trouble spots after
reviewing only 50 listings suggests a larger problem for our industry. Namely, that we are missing
opportunities.

Technology Improves Pixel Consistency, Pizzazz

A first step to correcting the pixel problems in this
chapter is a self-assessment. I would encourage
every dealer and used vehicle manager to take the
time to see how their inventory listings on third-
party sites stack up against other dealers in their
markets.

In suggesting this, I recognize why this exercise has
gone undone at many stores. It's a flat-out pain to
get vehicle photos and descriptions online in the

first place—let alone tweak the finer points of pixel proficiency.

A lack of time is not a good enough excuse to let such process and execution shortcomings undermine a store's profit potential because, make no mistake, these efforts will directly affect online traffic, showroom "ups," and, ultimately the bottom line.

Velocity dealerships use technology to audit their pixel proficiency and figure out why they may see drops in their SRPs and VDPs or their equivalents. This technology can spot inconsistencies in pricing and missing photos/videos/vehicle descriptions and offer alerts when these issues occur.

Joe Pistell, marketing director for *UsedCarKing.com,* which has three locations in upstate New York, noticed a lead-count drop from *Cars.com.* His lead averages were fine from *AutoTrader.com,* so he suspected a potential problem on the former site.

Using the tracking technology, Pistell found a 20 percent discrepancy between the number of photos on *Cars.com* compared with *AutoTrader.com* (184 units without photos). Technology allowed him to create and send a list of the vehicles and stock numbers to his Web team. It took him 30 minutes to create the list, and his team fixed the problem by the following day. His lead tallies subsequently picked up.

"Like every good manager, I make my rounds walking the online inventory," Pistell says. "I look around and see a missing picture here and there, but I'd *never* connect this to a larger problem. By far, that was the best 30 minutes I've spent in a long time. This technology saved me time and money."

In addition to audit technology, some velocity dealers and used vehicle managers also use technology to automate vehicle description-writing—another key time-saver.

"This changes the whole game of getting good descriptions," says a West Coast dealer who uses the tool.

The intent of this chapter is to underscore the importance of putting the time, energy, and effort into ensuring that all aspects of the pixel bait that consumers see on third-party sites bear the same kind of consistency and pristine look and feel that dealers and used vehicle managers work hard to achieve with their physical inventories every day.

If I was the dealer or used vehicle manager at the stores I spotted in my used vehicle searches, I would have a sizable to-do list for my pixel team.

Simply stated, it is no longer acceptable to allow inconsistencies and holes to erode the impact of online inventory listings. Photos and descriptions are far too important, and the screen real estate here is far too expensive and valuable, to publish what amounts to bush league pixel bait.

From what I can tell, virtually every dealer and used vehicle manager can and should do a better job on this front. It's really a choice of conviction to change or complacency.

Let's move into some examples of pixel proficiency done right.

Dialing Up "Pixel Proficiency"

Here's another chapter that needs a bit of explanation. While there is a lot of buzz about more sophisticated Internet marketing tactics that will be described below, I believe that dealers should defer taking action until they have mastered the basic pixel proficiencies outlined to this point.

Therefore, don't get too spun up on some of the heavy detail, just take what you need when needed.

For more than a decade, a soundproof booth played a key role in the advertising and marketing strategy for the Sam Swope Auto Group.

> *"We had a soundproof booth upstairs from the showroom. We'd always ask our customers, 'How much did you save?'" Swope explains. "We gave the customer $1 and they dutifully stated the amount of their saving. The salesman's reward was that we put his name in the ad."*

"We did testimonial advertising exclusively for 14 years," says Sam Swope, the 83-year-old first generation dealer who's built a powerhouse of 15 stores from the humble beginnings of a Dodge/Plymouth store he opened in 1952 in Elizabethtown, Kentucky.

"We had a soundproof booth upstairs from the showroom. We'd always ask our customers, 'How much did you save?'" Swope explains. "We gave the customer $1 and they dutifully stated the amount of their saving. The salesman's reward was that we put his name in the ad."

These days, however, it's a different kind of booth that plays a critical role in the advertising and marketing strategy for the Swope operation. This booth occupies the corner of a warehouse that houses the used vehicle detailing and touch-up shop, located about a quarter-mile from Swope's campus-like collection of stores.

It's an open-air space, with movable backdrops and light diffusers, and a 16'-diameter revolving platform in the center. The platform shows the tire tracks of vehicles that make their way up to sit for the 27 photos that will become a critical part of the pixel presentation for Swope's online used vehicle inventory.

Swope's director of used vehicle operations, Cary Donovan, says he's not done tweaking the booth's lighting, camera placements, and other technical specs. "I'm still working on the concept," he says. "There's no template for this."

And he's right. Across the country, dealerships are figuring out how best to showcase their used vehicles online and to do so in a manner that allows speed and control of the process. It's the desire for speed and control—and the efficiencies that come from both—that push some dealers and used vehicle managers to take a do-it-yourself (DIY) approach to handling the pixel processes of their online used vehicle merchandising and sales.

Craig Belowski also favors a DIY approach. He has cross-trained his Internet manager and salespeople to handle the photo-taking for when his part-time student photographer isn't available. They also know how to do touch-up work in Photoshop, an editing program. The store dedicates a delivery bay for photo-taking and seeks a unified look and feel for all of its used vehicles, with an average of 18 photos per vehicle.

"The photos are done consistently," Belowski says. "They're an important part of our process."

In many instances, trial and error plays a key role in the learning curve. The playbook for pixel proficiency is still being written and, as every dealer and used vehicle manager knows, advances in new technologies and online destinations seem to keep pushing the finish line further away.

A better way to think of pixel proficiency is to realize that there is no finish line. By its nature, online merchandising and marketing of used vehicles is evolutionary. What works today may be outdated by tomorrow. Such is the nature of today's technology-driven business environment, and the role the Internet plays in retailing used vehicles.

That's why a metrics-minded approach to managing and monitoring pixel proficiency is critical. Technology can change, but the metrics remain constant beacons for what works and what doesn't. It's like a boat on storm-whipped waters at night. The captain may not be able to see exactly what's coming, or even know for certain that all is well, but his compass provides the course for a safe return to port.

With that backdrop, let's take a closer look at the pixel-based processes that some velocity-minded dealers and used vehicle managers use to do a better job of online merchandising and marketing their used vehicle inventories.

PIXEL-BASED BEST PRACTICES
FOR ONLINE MERCHANDISING

As noted, photos of used vehicles are key elements of the pixel bait that can attract potential buyers to a dealership's online inventory. In addition to the DIY approaches that Donovan and Belowski use for taking photos, they also ensure this part of the pixel process doesn't delay their potential to make maximum gross profit.

Donovan strives for a 48- to 72-hour turnaround from the time a vehicle arrives at Swope to the time it is reconditioned, photographed, and posted online. This is a far faster turnaround rate than what occurs at many traditional dealerships.

In fact, at many of these stores, dealers and used vehicle managers aim for a 3-to-5-day turnaround, but the reality is closer to 7 to 10 days. At velocity stores where the average time in inventory is typically less than 25 days, a 10-day lag is an unacceptable delay that translates to lost profit potential.

At Finish Line Ford in Peoria, Ill., this kind of delay is unacceptable. Thanks to technology, Bill Pearson has at least one photo posted online within minutes of his acquisition of any used vehicle at auctions. He relies on back-end data transfers (including the stock photos from auctions and other sources) to post the unit to his DMS and get it online quickly.

A Personalized Pixel Approach

Here's a quick look at how one store does a little extra pixel work with customers.

Once a customer lead arrives, an Internet sales person calls and typically leaves a message. Next step: Send a biography on the vehicle that includes photos, Carfax report and directions to the dealership and a quote. They also send a custom, from-the-desk video that explains how the salesperson will handle his/her role in guiding and completing a deal.

After an appointment is set, salespeople then use flip phones they've purchased themselves to send a 60-second walk-around of the vehicle the customer likes.

The upshot: "Customers recognize that we're going out of our way to help," the store's e-commerce director says. "That's been the big difference for us."

"We can have the car online and for sale the same day or within 24 hours, even if it hasn't been through service," says Pearson, whose detailers and touch-up crews get paid for fast work as soon as a vehicle arrives on a transport. "If your car isn't online, it's not for sale."

Here are a few other pixel process nuggets to consider for photos:

Brand your store. This may be an obvious point, but some dealers and used vehicle managers overlook the branding opportunities that exist for their stores via store-logoed frames, backdrops, and license plate holders. In fact, there is new technology available that allows dealers to put a watermark on each and every photo.

Highlight the finer features. If the Market Days Supply reflects that a unit's sunroof, GPS, entertainment system, leather seats, or other features add to its value, it's important for photos to showcase these gems. Some dealers and used vehicle managers tweak the order of the photos they serve up on vehicles to give more prominence to these value-building add-ons.

Show your team. Few stores do this, but it strikes me as a nice touch. The photos show sales team members and speak to a store's "we'll take care of you" message.

Beyond photos, videos and descriptions play a key role in effective, pixel-smart online merchandising. Here's a brief look at both topics:

Vehicle videos: These are all the rage as consumers pay more attention to vehicles that include videos than those that only offer up pictures. It adds one more piece of pixel bait to the initial search listing pages online shoppers see when they hunt third-party sites for vehicles.

Typically, dealers and used vehicle managers include vehicle-focused videos that may be a collection of still photos, with an audio track. Other stores go a step further and create walk-around videos of the vehicle with audio from a member of the Internet or sales team.

Howard Polirer, director of industry relations for *AutoTrader.com* says video testimonials offer another credibility-building component to a dealer's pixel bait. The goal, he notes, is "why buy from me?" differentiation. "A lot of the obstacles with videos have been removed," says Polirer, referring to difficulties with uploads and customer load times.

It's important to note that videos also feed the online marketing aspects of a dealership's pixel proficiency. A growing number of dealers are using *YouTube* as the repository for storing their videos and providing link connections to and from their third-party site listings and dealership websites.

The purpose: To expand a store's online screen real estate and leverage the lift these online spaces can provide for a dealership's content when consumers use search engines to look for used vehicles and dealerships online.

"The key here," says automotive Internet marketing consultant Sean Bradley, "is the proper optimization and back-end keyword coding to make sure search engines see each video as different."

Vehicle descriptions: The biggest challenge for dealers and used vehicle managers, as noted in the last chapter, is creating a process that drives compelling vehicle descriptions that highlight the most valuable features of a vehicle in a time-efficient manner.

The time crunch is the main reason many dealers and used vehicle managers rely on the VIN decode/explosion option that populates the vehicle descriptions with the usual fare of equipment and features. The problem here is two-fold:

1. Many of the descriptions result in rote recitations of power steering, power brakes, and other features/equipment that many of today's buyers deem a given. Why use this valuable screen real estate and pixel bait on bland items such as these?

2. The descriptions do not play up the most salient and valuable features of a specific vehicle.

A point of efficiency: I've heard some stores charge the person who takes photos with writing descriptions, assuming the individual's got a solid knack for writing. Likewise, managers say it's helpful to keep a library of descriptions to feed creative comments on specific units.

John Creran sums up the coaching he provides to
a part-time, college student who writes descriptions: "I don't want to hear this is a low mileage,
clean, no-smoker car. Give it some life. Be funny. Be
creative. There are no boundaries. Stay away from
all the gray areas. Have fun with it."

There's a final take-away from the approaches Creran and other velocity-minded stores have adopted:
The job of writing vehicle descriptions likely falls
below the pay grade for most used vehicle managers. This will become increasingly true as today's
efficient used vehicle marketplace continues to put
margin pressure on dealerships that fail to adopt
more efficient and less costly pixel-based processes.

PIXEL-BASED BEST PRACTICES
FOR ONLINE MARKETING

When Auction Direct USA, an independent used
vehicle retailer with three stores in New York,
North Carolina, and Florida, opened for business
they crafted a compelling mission statement[16]:

> *"Auction Direct USA is committed to
> revolutionizing and legitimizing the used car
> business, guided by the principles of trust and
> open information exchange, to provide a truly
> unique and satisfying automotive purchase
> experience for every guest, in every way."*

---

[16]http://www.auctiondirectusa.com/dsp_about.cfm

The founders had a vision of building a brand around this mission statement and using both brick and mortar and online platforms to convey it.

On the brick and mortar side, the company's stores lack any offices. Showrooms have only one vehicle. A bar-style horseshoe serves as the focal point where customers and salespeople work out deals. Customers have access to computers to research or browse the Internet, whether they're buying a vehicle or not.

"If you weren't paying attention, you might not think you're in a car dealership," says Eric Miltsch, IT director and partner for the company, which retails about 700 vehicles per month across its three current locations. "It's a unique experience."

The company's pixel presence is similarly compelling. It conveys the company's core mission statement and underscores its "no hassle, no haggle" transparent style of retailing vehicles. It touts a three-day, 500-mile guarantee and clean-conscience certification on all vehicles.

More than that, though, Auction Direct is everywhere online: In *Google* search listings for used vehicles in its markets, in social media spaces such as *Facebook, Twitter,* and *YouTube,* and on third-party sites. Each of these online spaces links to the others, creating a spider web-like platform that supports itself and, through careful day-to-day management of the individual anchors, grows bigger over time.

I have always believed that consumers *prefer* to view a variety of listings from multiple dealers to shop for a vehicle that fits their budget and needs and, therefore, third-party sites like *AutoTrader.com* and *Cars.com* would be where dealers and used vehicle managers would connect best with shoppers.

At the same time, however, I recognize that many online shoppers get to these sites from search engines. My problem has been clearly understanding how dealerships can or should connect to this initial stage of the online shopping funnel and the value it may bring.

Miltsch and other velocity-minded dealers and used vehicle managers have helped educate me about how this works. It's not all about trying to position specific vehicles or deals within the organic listings that appear when consumers use a search engine. Instead, it's about demonstrating that a) a store has the vehicles and b) it understands consumers want selection and resources to guide their decisions.

For example, Miltsch optimizes his dealership's website to appear when someone types in "used vehicles NY." He's done the research to know the term is relevant and frequently used by shoppers. To optimize the page he wants to appear in search results, he makes sure the "used vehicles NY" appears in the page title and content on the page so search engine spiders view it as relevant to the online consumer's initial query.

The Auction Direct listing on this term that appears in search results (No. 5, when I checked) contains the keyword term and talks about the company's best used cars. A click-through goes to the home page that offers a search function that's similar to what a third-party site offers consumers.

Micro-sites also aid the efforts in gaining consumer attention in the search. Brian Benstock, Paragon Honda, has a host of sites—including a blog based on his name—that work together to drive traffic to his store's website. "We have a saying, 'go viral or go home,'" he says.

This summer his store joined an effort to follow the federal Cash for Clunkers program with a dealer-run plan that includes used vehicles. The effort ties Paragon and other dealers to a website, *www.autostimulusplan.com,* that seeks to capture customer interest in the federal program and offer up used vehicles it did not include.

"Cash for Clunkers applied to 10 percent of the population," Benstock says. "We think if we can tap into the 90 percent of the market that's out there, we think we can do monster business over the next 90 days."

OK. So this is starting to make sense. These guys are creating and optimizing content that appeals to a customer's interests based on keywords. At this stage, it's less about merchandising a specific vehicle and more about merchandising the dealership—making sure customers can see their stores as a viable choice to help them accomplish what they need—whether it's a vehicle purchase or resources to give them additional information around their search query.

"It's about understanding how search engines work," Miltsch says. "They reward you when you provide a site that has some type of valuable and relevant content that is linked to just as many valuable and highly authoritative, highly relevant content-related sites."

I had to ask the question: What about SEO and SEM for specific vehicles or deals?

In this case, Miltsch zeroes in on makes/models that are hot sellers, rather than trying to position specific vehicles in search listings. For example, if he knows "used Ford Explorer" is a common term, he'll optimize a search results page for Ford Explorers from his site to appear high in search listings. The idea: He knows shoppers will want to compare, so he serves up a page that offers immediate comparisons.

Miltsch and other velocity-minded stores also sprinkle their pixel-based online marketing with pay-per-click and display advertising to address more deal-specific messaging. Typically, these will complement other organic optimization efforts that seek to position dealership website pages in search engine results. The idea: the paid and organic listings complement each other and serve up messaging that's relevant to the potential customer's search query.

But Miltsch and others note this kind of optimization work isn't possible at all dealerships due to the frame-based website structures they use that are search-unfriendly.

The problem: The frame architecture that some dealer website developers use create pages within pages that search engine spiders have trouble reading and indexing for search results listings[17]. Likewise, these sites offer less flexibility to create/change search-friendly URLs for specific pages or to embed keywords in page content so that search engine spiders deem them relevant and rank them higher in search results listings.

"We did away with that framed-in solution and did our own to control our URL structure and create a canonical design to help our optimization efforts," Miltsch says.

---

[17] http://www.seonotepad.com/seo/seo-and-html-frames/

Chris Fousek, e-commerce director at Village Auto Group, Boston, agrees frame-based sites are problematic. "Framed inventory detracts from your whole site," he says. "We're focused on text-based sites to help us in search."

Dean Evans, chief marketing officer for *Dealer.com*, says the problem of frame-based sites is one that stems from dealers and site developers aiming for flashy presentations over search-friendly functionality. The pendulum is shifting but Evans notes some dealers still opt for sites and SEO programs based on a good sales pitch rather than a clear track record of improving search results listings and traffic gains for dealerships.

A key take-away: Dealers and used vehicle managers who are unfamiliar with the ins and outs of SEO and SEM should make sure their websites are at least set up to allow this kind of marketing to support their pixel proficiency.

In addition to optimizing their own sites, some dealers and used vehicle managers are embracing other online marketing tactics to build and manage their online presence:

> **Reputation management.** A growing number of dealers and used vehicle managers are investing time and energy to encourage customer reviews on sites that rate dealerships—these include *Dealer Rater, Google Local, Yelp,* and

Citysearch sites. Joe Orr, GM for Dick Hannah Dealerships, Portland, Ore., says salespeople encourage customers to make comments on these sites. After a year-long concerted effort, the dealership has tracked more than 460 "ups" for sales, service, and parts—incremental business that flowed directly from the listings (more than 700 in '08) on the review sites.

These are free calls compared to leads from other sites, Orr says. In addition, because the store is more aware of managing customers' online feedback, salespeople are more focused on their satisfaction. CSI ratings have climbed about 2 points higher in the past year as Dick Hannah stores have made online reputation management a higher priority.

"People read this stuff. It works," echoes John Creran. He's focused on positive listings on *Dealer Rater.*

Of course, these online reviews carry risks of negative comments from customers. The best practice here: Do everything possible to contact customers and resolve complaints, and address those outcomes in responses to online complaints. This provides balance to any misinformation or misconceptions conveyed in the complaints.

One benefit of a concerted focus on positive listings: The sites typically post comments from most recent to older reviews. So, in time, negative comments get pushed down and counter-balanced by more favorable reviews.

"We're confident we can get past a couple of bad reviews," says Belowski at Acton Toyota.

Social Media Spaces: More dealers and used vehicle managers are engaging social media spaces like *YouTube, Facebook,* and *Twitter* to further connect their stores with the online spaces where past and potential customers congregate.

"That's where people are, so our strategy is to go there and not try to pull them away," Miltsch says.

Auction Direct's messaging and discussion in these spaces is not about selling cars. Rather, they skew toward topics that automotive enthusiasts might find compelling—whether it's tips on purchasing a car, discussions about new models, or warnings about the dangers of using cell phones while driving.

"After two or three years' worth of effort, we have actually sold vehicles from those channels," Miltsch says. "It's helped maintain relationships, drive traffic, and build the brand."

DrivingSales.com founder Jared Hamilton says social media spaces should not be any big mystery to dealers. Participation in these spaces is much like the memberships in the Rotary Club and chamber of commerce and sponsorship of Little League teams. They generate good will and, occasionally, they may make a connection that leads to a deal.

These spaces can also be channels for fun stuff, like customer-generated videos. Auction Direct invited customers to create their own commercial for the company, offering a $5,000 award for the best one.

"We got 25 goofy videos. We keep them there. They keep getting views," says Miltsch, who notes *YouTube* also holds the active TV commercials the store runs in its markets.

Automotive Internet consultant Sean Bradley notes that spaces like *YouTube* are increasingly becoming go-to places where online consumers search for information, much like they do on *Google* or *Yahoo*.

The upshot: Online videos should be optimized to connect with the keywords that consumers might use when they look for videos. Bradley notes this includes knowing the keyword terms that matter most and embedding those terms in video titles, descriptions, and tags—the elements of optimization.

A MOMENT OF INTERNET MARKETING LEVITY

We could go on and on about the potential opportunities that exist for dealers and used vehicle managers when it comes to building their brands and screen real estate.

As I'm writing, real-time chats and mobile phone technologies appear as two emerging areas of online marketing that dealers and used vehicle managers will likely need to address in the near future.

It's potentially overwhelming and is a far cry from the way our business has been for much of the past century.

The key here is setting priorities. It would be a mistake to chase all these online marketing opportunities without a clear strategy and a sustained degree of pixel proficiency across the online spaces where, for the most part, the bulk of the current action occurs—namely, the third-party sites and dealers' own websites.

As Mitch Golub says, there's a danger of "stepping over $20 bills to pick up dimes" for dealers and used vehicle managers who skip past the fundamentals of pixel proficiency and beat a fast path to cash in on the buzz that surrounds social media spaces and other online marketing channels.

Hamilton at *DrivingSales.com* agrees. "The easiest starting place is the online classifieds. There is no primary skill that's needed for your sales staff to take advantage of those leads, unlike the specialized skills for search optimization and marketing," he says. "You've got to have someone that knows how to price and take the pictures and knows how to write descriptions."

Perfecting this degree of pixel proficiency is the critical point of entry that leads to more robust e-endeavors that seek to make a dealership's website the primary catch-point for all online marketing activities.

"The dealership website is an extension of their store," Hamilton says. "If you want your website to be a marketing arm for you, you have to get into search engine marketing, search engine optimization, and other things to drive traffic to your site. Then, the way you manage your website is through conversion rates. Its job is to convert traffic to leads."

HOW VELOCITY PRINCIPLES BOOST PROFITABILITY

Brian Benstock of Paragon Honda took a big gamble in 2007.

The store had been spending $100,000 a month on newspaper advertising to spur used vehicle sales. But Benstock had seen floor traffic diminish and, when the contract with one of the city's top papers came up for renewal, he sought a reduced rate.

"The ad rep, who has since been fired, wasn't being flexible," Benstock says. "So, I called his bluff and cancelled our contract."

That decision triggered a new focus at the dealership: using the Internet as its chief marketing channel to build used vehicles sales.

At the same time, Benstock knew he had a problem. The store was land-locked, which meant his desire to grow used vehicle volumes could not come on the back of a larger investment in inventory. He simply didn't have the room.

His solution came with the adoption of velocity-minded management principles and technology and a more efficiency-focused strategy.

"Our focus went from dollars per unit to dollars per day per space," Benstock says. "The dollars per unit focus meant we were trying to make $3,000 a car no matter how long it took. We might take up that real estate for 90 days to get that $3,000.

"When we started looking at dollars per day per space, we said, 'Perhaps in that 90 days if we made $1,000 on the car and could turn that space four times or more in 90 days, we'd be better off,'" he says.

"It didn't take a genius to figure out that four turns of $1,000 was better than one turn of $3,000. And when you add in all the components—the service, F&I, and aftermarket opportunities—the $1,000 actually ends up being more like $2,500."

Paragon stats suggest Benstock's gamble has paid off. "Our used business has doubled and doubled again to 300 units a month. We turn our inventory 15 to 16 times a year," he says. Meanwhile, the store's average advertising cost-per-vehicle has dropped about 50 percent to $240. Much of that spend goes to ongoing costs to seed and feed the store's formidable Web presence.

These gains come on top of a reduced, front-end gross profit average on the sale of each vehicle— something that might have once rubbed Benstock the wrong way.

"I used to be the highest average grossing used car dealer," he says. "Now I just make the most money. It's a complete paradigm shift and it's one that will make you rich."

So go the benefits of a used vehicle management strategy that focuses on velocity and efficiency. In today's used vehicle marketplace, where the enhanced knowledge of Internet buyers and the rising costs of running a business create new margin pressures, it's essential for dealerships to focus on ways to reduce costs, improve turn rates, and build profitability.

For some traditional dealers and used vehicle managers, Benstock's success is a head-scratcher. They intuitively understand that a faster rate of turn can

yield greater ROI, but they question whether veloc-
ity- and efficiency-minded processes can actually
result in store- and lifestyle-sustaining profits.

The difficulty in seeing the profit potential is understandable. Since its inception, our business has
focused on gross profits per vehicle retailed (PVR).
This affects everything dealers and used vehicle
managers do—they price vehicles (e.g., the $4,000
to $5,000 mark-up-from-cost) and sell vehicles (e.g.,
four-square, shell game-like processes) to achieve
maximum PVR on every unit.

By contrast, Benstock and other velocity dealers go
a different route. They strive for efficiency in pricing vehicles to their markets and selling vehicles
in a transparent manner that consistently reflects
the information their customers have already seen
on the Internet. This approach leaves PVR by the
wayside. For traditional dealers who struggle to
see the value in efficiency- and velocity-minded
management, let's take a closer look at some of the
reasons why velocity dealers like Benstock can still
achieve respectable PVRs and why the overall gains
in net profits for their stores typically outpace those
of the competition.

THE "RACE TO THE BOTTOM" MYTH

Traditional dealers and managers often express their concern about the profitability that can flow from a velocity approach to used vehicle management with the following question:

> *"If everybody started doing this, wouldn't it create a 'race to the bottom' where dealerships sell more vehicles but nobody's making any money because everyone's selling at the lowest price possible?"*

The question's completely fair, but it misses the mechanics of how efficient markets work, and the innate opportunities these markets create for astute players who look for them.

As noted in earlier chapters, today's used vehicle marketplace meets the definition of an efficient market—one where there's equal knowledge of choices and alternatives between buyers and sellers, and the dynamics of supply and demand determine the selling prices of products.

Traditional commodities markets, such as grain, oil, cattle, etc., meet this definition. These markets create winners and losers every day, and sometimes they're the same individual(s).

Investors in these markets carefully attune their buying and selling to account for supply and demand dynamics and the return they can expect from commodity prices on a given day. So, if the market for corn softens because of high supply and low demand, these investors will likely shift their focus to another market where the prospect for a return on their investment is brighter. As these investors exit the corn market, its dynamics shift. In time, the supply and demand swings level off and re-attract investors who opted out previously.

These are the kinds of market dynamics that velocity dealerships dial into every day. If the market softens for SUVs, the savvy market-attuned velocity-minded stores will shift their attention to vehicle segments where Market Days Supply, Price to Market and Cost to Market metrics offer a more favorable potential ROI for their respective stores.

Just like hot-and-cold commodities markets, today's more volatile used vehicle business offers up market segments that can be winners one day and losers the next. It's through seeing such market shifts that velocity dealers adjust their inventories to capture the profit sweet spots across vehicle segments, and reduce their exposure to risk by eliminating vehicles that have turned into losers. It's not uncommon for velocity stores that have long considered themselves truck or SUV specialists to broaden their inventories and give more attention to other vehicle types their markets crave.

"If you're on a 15-day turn, you can get out of the pain much quicker than somebody who's on a slower turn," Benstock says. "You react quicker to the market."

When it comes to pricing, these market sweet spots typically offer higher PVR potential. Velocity dealers leverage this knowledge to achieve the maximum gross profit the market will bear from the moment they acquire these units. (Note: Some velocity dealers may "skinny up" their PVR expectations to turn a vehicle faster, and sell a second or third unit that falls in the sweet spot.)

In any case, these velocity stores will avoid a mark-up-from-cost approach to setting their retail asking prices. Their goal is to "meet" rather than "make" the market. To do so, they'll tune into the paint metrics to determine the appropriate price point that will yield the best PVR and their store's business goals, based on the vehicle's condition, mileage, and trim/equipment configuration.

So the race isn't toward the bottom, it's a race to:

- Understand the efficient market's equilibrium points—those moments that occur in vehicle segments when the market is ripe for acquiring and retailing specific types of units, given high demand or low supply;

- Find these vehicles more quickly and more efficiently than the competition;

- Identify the moments when the market starts to rot on a given vehicle, given shifts in supply and demand dynamics;

- Make stocking and pricing decisions that accurately reflect ripe and rot stages of individual vehicles in a market.

STORE-WIDE PROFIT AND SAVINGS POTENTIAL

As I've studied the successes of velocity dealers like Benstock, it's amazing to see the trickle-down benefits that come to dealerships that adopt velocity management principles.

The focus on more cost-effective and efficient operations translates to bottom line benefits that outperform those seen at traditional stores—even if they are fortunate enough to have a steady stream of buyers who lay down on deals with sizable PVRs.

These benefits flow directly from faster turns and lower operating costs in the used vehicle departments, and they reflect the profit-positive outcomes that well-managed and well-executed paint and pixel processes generate.

In prior chapters, we've noted how faster turn rates on used vehicles increase revenue and profit opportunities in service and F&I. I would consider these direct rather than trickle-down benefits, as they flow in kind from a greater degree of activity in the used vehicle department.

The trickle-down benefits are those that are less easy to spot. They come in the form of reduced operating costs and greater efficiencies velocity stores achieve when they focus on and perfect their paint and pixel processes.

The following chart highlights the cost savings that trickle down to used vehicle departments at velocity stores—on top of the direct gains they enjoy from increased sales volumes. The chart compares typical expenses at tradition dealerships and velocity-minded stores.

All of these benefits—savings on floor plan, advertising, and compensation—result from the fact that velocity stores focus on finding the market's sweet spots that ensure fast inventory turn and maximum ROI. This approach reduces exposure to the costs of holding on to inventory, spiffing sales teams, and advertising spending that traditional dealerships typically pay as they wait for willing buyers.

When I share these financial benefits with skeptical dealers and used vehicle managers, they start to understand why a velocity approach to used vehicle management is much, much more than a race to the bottom. It is, in fact, a race to a more profit-favorable bottom line.

Financial Benefits			
	Traditional	Velocity	Savings
Comp Dollars per Retail	$627	$474	$153
Total Comp as a % of Retail Gross	25.5%	22.5%	3.0%
Advertising Dollars per Retail	$322	$189	$133
Advertising as % of Retail Gross	17.9%	12.2%	5.7%
Floor Plan	$53	$23	$30
As a % of Used Vehicle Gross	2.9%	1.5%	1.4%
Total Used Selling Expense per Retail	$1,083	$765	$318
Total Used Selling Expense % of Gross	44.2%	36.7%	7.5%

Dealers like Jon Whitman say the adoption of a velocity-based management philosophy has helped his store thrive, rather than just survive.

Whitman's dealership is located in southeast Michigan where the unemployment rate runs 20 percent and new jobs are not likely to appear anytime soon given the region's dependence on automotive manufacturers.

"If I had to depend on my town to survive, I wouldn't be here," Whitman says. "I'm not complaining. It is what it is. I just have to deal with it, be more efficient, and do the best I can with the tools and technology I have at my disposal."

Implementing a combination of paint-based metrics and pixel proficiency has helped Whitman expand his dealership's market area and sell a greater number of used vehicles than ever before.

All of a sudden you start realizing, "I don't want to make a lot of money on this car. I don't want to marry it. I don't want to date it long. I want to have it come here, get a reasonable ROI as quickly as possible, and move on to the next one."

"The guy who buys my vehicle is sitting three hours away. He's coming to me from towns with names I can't even spell, because I've never heard of them," he says.

As Whitman and other dealers and used vehicle managers adopt and deploy velocity-based processes, I'm absolutely convinced that they will succeed at the expense of traditional dealerships.

I like Benstock's "broken record" take on this: "The more turn you have, the fresher your inventory; the fresher your inventory the more turn; and the more turn, the fresher your inventory," he says. "It gets crazy. All of a sudden you start realizing I don't want to make a lot of money on this car. I don't want to marry it. I don't want to date it long. I want to have it come here, get a reasonable ROI as quickly as possible, and move on to the next one."

One final point about the trickle-down, profit-driving benefits of velocity-based principles: The figures shared here are based on the early experiences of velocity-minded stores. As noted in prior chapters, many are currently tweaking their paint and pixel processes to achieve an even greater degree of efficiency and profitability.

In evaluating the moves these velocity dealers and used vehicle managers are making, it's become clear that a new structure for variable operations at dealerships may well deliver an even greater degree of efficiency and profitability.

A Case for "Efficient," Profitable Variable Operations

It's striking to see the variations in approach and process that dealerships have taken as they embrace the Internet's role in retailing new and used vehicles.

Here are three common models:

The BDC: Some stores rely on business development centers (BDCs) as the hub to receive and tracks calls and emails that flow from online used vehicle listings. In many cases, the BDC teams set appointments on behalf of salespeople. Sometimes, dealerships put salespeople in BDC areas for mandatory, rotating shifts.[18] It's not uncommon for BDCs to handle all incoming communications, including sales, service, and parts.

Stand-alone Internet Departments: These departments are the designated hitters for incoming leads (calls, emails, and other queries) that flow from third-party listing and lead generation sites. Typically, these teams include salespeople who have little traditional showroom-selling experience. On occasion, these teams also include salespeople who have proven their showroom skills, and earn the chance to take fresh "ups" from online sources.

Integrated Internet Selling: This model is often born from unsuccessful attempts by dealers and used vehicle managers to make the previous models work. The idea is that every salesperson should be able and equipped to handle any customer, whether they come from Internet sources or more traditional channels. These salespeople handle all leads, appointment-setting, and other work needed to capture and close customers.

Out of these three, it's difficult to call one a clear winner in terms of effectiveness. In my travels and

---

[18] The inclusion of salespeople at BDCs has given rise to derogatory terms like "Business Detention Centers," which makes this approach one of the more difficult to run successfully.

speaking at industry conferences on the Internet and automotive retailing, each of the three is or has been described as the best approach for today's dealerships.

In addition, there are probably a half-dozen other hybrid approaches that flow from these basic models—sometimes incorporating tasks necessary for effective online merchandising and sometimes relegating those duties to managers who also handle desking and inventory management responsibilities.

What's going on here? It's nothing short of today's franchised automotive retailers trying to figure out the best way to address the role the Internet plays as a chief conduit for their sales operations.

There isn't a job today in the variable operations at dealerships that isn't somehow connected to the Internet—whether it's the branding and marketing of a store, the online merchandising of new and used vehicles, the tracking and management of new/used sales leads, or the sourcing of new/used vehicle inventories. Put another way, there's a darn good reason why there's a computer on every desk.

But our industry's quest to find a solution is hampered by our past.

We don't have TV departments

I should come clean on one of my biases: I've never thought that a stand-alone Internet department made sense from a managing the overall business perspective.

In effect, stand-alone departments splinter a customer base that, for all intents and purposes, is the same. All buyers use the Internet.

The Internet is a marketing channel similar to other mediums, such as radio, cable and broadcast TV.

In the past, dealerships never created stand-alone TV, radio or newspaper departments to manage leads or "ups" from these channels.

I understand why stand-alone Internet departments came into being. I firmly believe, however, their time has come and, in the not-so-distant future, they will be relics.

As I see it, dealers are either:

1. Bolting Internet-related tasks and responsibilities onto existing new and used vehicle departments, a shift that can place responsibility for pixel proficiency in the hands of people who are more paint-savvy; or

2. Creating separate layers of people and processes to manage Internet-driven business because existing managers and salespeople aren't up to the task.

This invites dysfunction and cost inefficiencies—neither of which any store can afford in today's more fast-moving, efficient and volatile marketplace.

This is the backdrop that has led me to ruminate on a key question: What's the best way to most efficiently and profitably serve today's Internet-enabled customers and effectively manage the paint and pixel proficiency that's a necessity for every dealership?

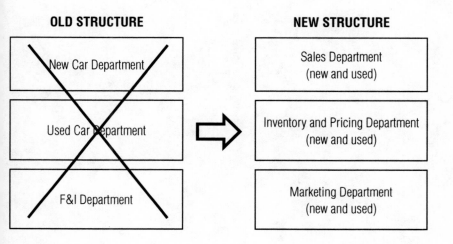

OLD STRUCTURE

- New Car Department
- Used Car Department
- F&I Department

NEW STRUCTURE

- Sales Department (new and used)
- Inventory and Pricing Department (new and used)
- Marketing Department (new and used)

As I've studied the ways velocity-minded dealers and used vehicle managers are working to answer it for themselves, I've arrived at a structure for the variable operations of dealerships that appears to be best suited to addressing the critical needs for paint and pixel proficiency, as well as profitability, that today's more efficient market requires.

At its core, this new structure recognizes that the Internet is the single most important driver for all vehicles sales—not just used—and puts the all-important pixel-related tasks in the hands of people who are innately wired to effectively and efficiently do them well. Put another way, it's time for the old structure variable operations to be replaced by one that is more functional and tailored to the times.

THE SALES DEPARTMENT

For 57 years, every Monday morning sales meeting at the Sam Swope Auto Group starts with a discussion of used vehicles.

"We are not a new car dealer with a used car department," says Sam Swope, the 83-year-old founder of the 15-store group. "We are used car dealers who, in most cases, happen to have a new car franchise."

Swope's stores consistently average a 2-plus to 1 ratio of used to new vehicle sales. It's a track record born of the recognition that he, as the dealer, controls his destiny in used vehicles—from picking what to sell to setting the price. Swope understands that the opportunities in used vehicles are rich, and they merit a more primary degree of attention than most dealerships give them.

"If you're trying to make it only on new cars and sell the trade-ins as they come in, the used vehicle department is a stepchild," he says.

Can I just say how much I love this business? Where else could a blind guy get a chance to talk to an auto retailing master like Swope? This guy isn't ahead of the curve; he helped create it!

Forgive me. I'm just struck by Sam Swope's philosophy. He didn't go the route of many of his first generation peers, who put a greater emphasis on new vehicles at the expense of used. Here we are, 60 years later, and the consequences of this backseat status for used vehicles are coming home to roost for too many dealerships.

Meantime, Sam Swope is out riding his motorcycle across the country. He's got guys like Dick Swope and Cary Donovan carrying on the used vehicle tradition. "The secret is to surround yourself with guys who are a lot smarter than you are," Swope says. "I don't have much trouble doing that."

See what I mean about a master? The pearls of wisdom fall like rain. Thank you, Mr. Swope.

A SINGLE SALES TEAM

Given the costs in people and processes to run separate new and used sales departments in addition to stand-alone Internet departments at some stores, it makes sense for dealerships to combine the new and used car departments.

After all, new and used customers shop online with equal energy and aplomb and, in today's credit-challenged environment, the best deal for a customer may well be a used vehicle, or vice versa, regardless of what vehicle the customer thought they might buy when they contacted the dealership.

Also, today's new and used vehicles are not as different from one another as they were in the past. Basically, selling a car, new or used, requires the same skills of meeting, greeting, qualifying, demoing, presenting price, and asking for the order. Moreover, today's used car is likely to be a highly reconditioned, possibly certified vehicle with some manufacturer's warranty that requires little if any creative and artful apologies to get it out the door. While there are still differences between selling new and used cars, the gap is simply not large enough to justify the overhead and expense of separate new and used car sales forces and management staffs.

As I've discussed the idea of a single sales department with velocity dealers and managers, they immediately see the potential cost savings and efficiencies a single team of Internet- and customer-savvy salespeople would deliver for a store.

But implementation of the idea is another matter, particularly as velocity dealers and managers assess their current sales teams and their ability to adjust to the new processes and roles that would be essential under a single sales department.

This is especially true in used vehicles, where the "hold 'em and fold 'em" style of selling has long been deemed a best practice and the Internet has leveled the playing field between dealers and customers. Many used vehicle departments at traditional stores still pay good negotiator salespeople top commissions for their ability to close customers.

By contrast, velocity dealers are sensing that negotiation skills are less essential when they tune their inventory and pricing to market metrics and move away from sales models that aim solely for maximum gross profits on every deal.

As we've noted, holding gross is still important, but it's on equal footing with a transparent, open-book type of transaction that uses market data to justify pricing and value. Put another way, salespeople at these stores have nothing to apologize for with the vehicles and pricing they're selling to customers.

The type of salesperson who fits best in this new process—call him "Salesman Sam"—is one who has a people-focused personality and a knack for keeping up with updates to CRM systems and ongoing contact with customers. It's also true, as we've noted in earlier chapters, that these individuals work well under pay plans that are based more on salary/volume rather than commission.

As I'm writing, the Dick Hannah Dealerships have taken what it hopes will be an initial step toward a single sales department that serves all customers, regardless of the sales channel that landed them on a vehicle or whether they are shopping for new or used.

GM Joe Orr says this transition has two key components:

1. An hourly wage-based pay plan. The plan offers $15/hour for 10 vehicles in a month and climbs to $25/hour for 20 or more vehicles.

2. A different breed of salesperson. Orr says the pay plan's intended to attract a more responsible and educated salesperson who has been socially conditioned to seek out hourly wages and follow processes that are critical to the success of any organization.

This initial step toward a unified sales department comes as Orr's four stores still retain separate Internet sales teams. He plans to offer a transition period to sales team members and it's entirely possible some salespeople will leave. Orr notes that the online posting of the initial help wanted ad drew 16 applicants in less than two hours.

"We're tired of pushing and pulling salespeople to do the processes that ensure success and let them enjoy ongoing business from loyal customers," Orr says. "Many salespeople think they get paid for getting a 'yes' and the job requires more than that.

"Our commitment to transferring our dealership group to a full Internet dealership that doesn't separate brick and mortar and digital will take a while," he continues.

Orr is not the only one who sees dealerships evolving toward a single sales department that place all customers—Internet and otherwise—in the hands of a sales team that's qualified to serve them. The prediction: Stand-alone Internet departments will go by the wayside.

"It's just a question of how fast it will happen," says Jared Hamilton, CEO and founder of *DrivingSales.com*. "The good dealers will get there faster than others, and some are already there. The fact is, you have 90 percent of customers starting online and you have 10 percent of your sales staff handling that medium. That just doesn't make any sense."

I would be remiss in this section if I didn't include a contrary view. At Toyota Sunnyvale, Adam Simms purposely has a direct sales team that handles all incoming Internet leads and a showroom team to handle walk-ins. His thinking: Today's customers use email, phone calls, text messages, and other ways to contact stores—a variety of channels that requires a level of time and attention that makes it impossible to charge a single team with these responsibilities and handling walk-in traffic.

Simms takes great pains to ensure his showroom team recognizes, respects, and responds to the online shopping customers have conducted before they arrive at the store. "Most customers transition to the physical, walk-in pathway," he says. "To collapse these two teams into one doesn't make sense to me."

I respect his viewpoint and see its merits. However, Simms' approach is still more nuanced than the Internet/traditional sales structures at most dealerships—particularly in his sweat-the-details approach to ensuring that his showroom team is technically savvy.

NEW ROLES FOR MANAGERS

One of the consequences of the back-seat status of the used vehicle departments at many dealerships is that while the business has grown more varied, complex, and volatile, its management has largely remained static. The traditional best practices for management often remain in place, and the to-do list keeps lengthening.

The "Used Car Joes" of our business have a whole lot more to worry about than they ever did. What's more, as many used vehicle managers like Joe struggle to keep up, they end up being less effective at everything they do.

There's an inherent mismatch. Joe is sometimes a talented negotiator and/or closer. Joe is sometimes a paint specialist. Joe is sometimes good with computers. Joe is sometimes good at managing sales teams. Joe is sometimes good at handling inventory and pricing decisions. Joe is sometimes good at managing reconditioning and detailing processes. Joe sometimes understands pixels.

"To Do List"

Check storefront · Lot maintenance · Website management

Certification responsibility · Window sticker management · Respond to internet leads

Log internet leads · Hiring · Appraisals · Online pricing

Validate URLs · Manage inbound calls · Training · TOs · SEM, SEO, PPC

Website navigation · Scheduling · Desk management · Vendor

relationships · Online advertising · Wholesale acquisition · Classified promotions · Daily

work plans · Cost per lead · Wholesale disposition · Manage

photos · CRM management · Compensation · F&I · Counting ups

Working deals · Counting calls · Reconditioning · Manage descriptions

Lot pricing · Publish prices · Background checks

When one considers the complexity of today's used vehicle manager's roles and responsibilities, particularly in light of the Internet's role in used vehicle retailing, is it possible that a single person has the skills and temerity to do all this well? The answer is obviously "no."

This realization leads me to two conclusions:

> First, it is longer feasible to simply hire a great used car manager like Joe and say, "Okay Tiger, go get the job done."

> Second, the job of the used vehicle manager needs an overhaul. Under this new sales department structure, Joe would be slotted in a role that suits his/her skill set and interests the best.

At some stores, Joe might best function as a kind of operations manager who oversees the processes that ensure paint and pixel proficiency and profitability. At other stores, Joe might work best as a desk manager who handles deals and customers, or he/she might handle sales team management functions, assuming there's an innate ability to provide the kind of nurturing management that individuals like "Salesman Sam" need to perform at their peak.

Suffice it to say, this single sales department would require significant up-front effort by dealers and managers to define the processes and tasks that are critical for success and match these to individuals who are best suited to perform them well.

Brian Benstock recently made the move to a single sales department where each salesperson handles any deal or customer, and he's divvied up the role of used car manager.

"At my Acura store, I no longer have a used car manager," Benstock says. "I no longer have a used car staff. I have product specialists. They can do what's best for our customer. At the end of the day, what's best for the customer is best for the dealership."

THE INVENTORY AND PRICING DEPARTMENT

I hesitate to even refer to this second new department as a department because, for many dealerships, it might involve a single or even part-time employee that stocks and prices for both new and used vehicles. This person might even be Joe, whose job changed under the new sales department structure detailed in the last chapter.

Why does placing the responsibility for stocking and pricing vehicles in the hands of specialists make sense? It's because the used car market is as efficient as the new vehicle market and the fundamentals behind stocking and pricing for new and used are essentially the same.

The goals of this department (or individual) are to stock new and used vehicles that have the highest demand and least supply, and to price and appraise these vehicles based on their individual physical qualities and respective price sensitivities based on real-time market dynamics. While the tools needed for performing these tasks may differ somewhat for new and used vehicles, the guiding principles for stocking, pricing, and appraising are identical.

Currently, most traditional dealerships split the management of new and used vehicle inventories between their respective department managers. This split used to make sense—used vehicles were different than new vehicles, and they required someone with traditional paint skills to manage them.

This split does not hold as much weight as it once did, given the shared efficiencies in new and used markets, and the identical skills needed to follow assessments of supply and demand data and dynamics in a dealer's market area.

The idea for this department is also supported by the steps many velocity dealers and used vehicle managers are already taking to address the more time-intensive needs of acquiring, stocking, and pricing the right vehicles for their used vehicle inventories.

Enter "Duane the Stocking and Pricing Guy." He would be the workhorse in this new, inventory and pricing department. He's got a gift for understanding technology and interpreting market data to make informed decisions on what to stock and sell in a dealership's market. He would work closely with the manager of the single sales department, as well as "Used Car Joe" to find, acquire, and price the inventories that are right for a store.

As noted, some velocity dealerships have already moved toward a centralized inventory management operation. They've appointed inventory specialists like Duane to work in conjunction with Joe and other managers to right-size both new and used inventories for their dealerships.

This single inventory and pricing department would likely have its most profound impact on used vehicle operations—where Joe often lacks the time and/or interest to aggressively hunt online to source vehicles and mine market-based paint metric data to determine the best vehicles to stock.

Duane would also help eliminate other inventory management dysfunctions that are all too common at many of today's traditional dealerships such as the following:

- **Reliance on past history.** Many stores look to what they've sold in the past to guide their stocking decisions. The problem: This is only useful as a starting point. Notions of core inventory often miss opportunities that deal-

erships have not tested, due in part to biases
Joe brings to the table about what works at a
store. Duane would challenge those biases and
let market-based metrics determine the inventory that's truly right for a store.

Today's used vehicle market moves so fast,
"what happened eight, nine, or ten months ago
might not matter," observes George Gabriel,
head of Gabriel & Associates, a dealership
consultant who specializes in used vehicle
department and sales process training. "Dealers need to reach out beyond what they call
their 'core' and maximize their opportunities
based on market data."

- **A "franchise-first" mentality.** We've already
  discussed how velocity-minded dealers and
  used vehicle managers are adjusting their
  inventory mixes to a roughly 50/50 split
  between franchise and off-brand vehicles. The
  market-based data Duane uses to guide inventory management would help a store achieve
  its optimal inventory mix and alleviate the
  biases that lead to inventory that's often too
  heavy in a single brand.

- **Emotional bonds to vehicles.** At many traditional stores, it's not uncommon for Joe to
  hold on to an aging vehicle because he made
  the initial decision to stock it and believes
  he'll find a buyer who's willing to pay up

to meet the gross profit expectations he set on the vehicle. In reality, this practice delays the recognition that Joe might have made a mistake. What's more, the decision to keep a vehicle prevents the store from replacing the aging unit with one that may deliver a faster turn on the store's investment and offer better ROI potential. Duane would take such emotional bonds out of the initial stocking decisions by setting market-based parameters for what to purchase and how much to pay for auction and trade-in vehicles. Likewise, Duane would make it easier for managers to let go of aging units that have lost their ROI potential. He'd be the guy responsible for monitoring the point at which a vehicle's inventory age saps its ROI potential and signals it's time to move on.

- **"Reflexive" pricing.** Duane would be wired into technology-driven metrics like Market Days Supply, Price to Market and Cost to Market. Through this data, he'd be able to ID the correct acquisition prices for vehicles and know, up front, what retail asking prices are competitive for a dealership's market. Of course, a manager would need to approve these pricing recommendations but this process would eliminate the "mark-up-from-cost" approach currently in use—a method that often results in vehicles being priced above the market for competing vehicles or, even worse, way too low for a vehicle that we stole.

- Appraisal tension. At many traditional dealerships, it's not uncommon for used vehicle departments to play second fiddle to new vehicle departments on appraisals. With a single inventory department, the market-based values that Duane provides would offer a more objective trade-in value that's fair to both the customer and the dealership.

With an Inventory and Pricing department, staffed with an individual such as Duane, I am confident of better stocking and pricing decisions that will be rendered with lower costs as well as greater speed and efficiencies.

THE MARKETING DEPARTMENT

With the Internet playing a more centralized role in the marketing of new and used vehicles, as well as service, parts, and the dealership as a whole, it makes sense to structure a marketing department around this paradigm-shifting medium.

A single marketing department would eliminate many of the inefficiencies at dealerships where new and used vehicle managers, and service and parts managers, often handle marketing and promotions for their respective departments. At the same time, a GM or dealer typically manages marketing of the store as a whole. In some instances, dealerships hire an outside agency to assist with overall marketing, often working in conjunction with dealers, GMs and individual department managers.

In all this, the oversight of online merchandising and marketing is more diffuse: New vehicle managers might handle online merchandising of new vehicle inventories, and used vehicle managers might handle the pixel proficiency for their inventories. Meanwhile, an Internet department or an e-commerce director might be responsible for managing online merchandising of new/used vehicles, as well as maintaining the store's online presence and marketing campaigns through its websites and emerging social media spaces.

To me, a single department, overseen by a GM or e-commerce-type director, offers a more effective approach to leveraging the power of the Internet as a critical branding and marketing channel for dealerships.

The department workhorse would be someone like "Digital Debbie," who has the aptitude and interest to juggle the multiple tasks associated with a store's pixel proficiency and guide the ever-growing online presence and engagement with today's customers through a dealership's website, social media channels, and online marketing campaigns.

Debbie would be the centralized hub for the pixel proficiency, overseeing the effectiveness of processes for creating and uploading vehicle descriptions, photos, and videos on third-party inventory sites. She'd track pixel metrics and feed her "what's working/not working" insights to managers in sales, inventory management, and other departments. She'd be responsible for assessing the ROI for online marketing campaigns and relationships with lead providers and third-party inventory listing sites.

Debbie would also have a keen understanding of SEM and SEO. She'd handle the job of lacing relevant keywords into website pages and online advertising campaigns to ensure greater visibility for her dealership. She'd know how to oversee the build-out of new web pages and sites, if not the ability to do this creative work herself.

Because Debbie lives for this kind of work, I suspect she would be far more efficient at these tasks than the people who hold these responsibilities today. In many cases, a store's pixel proficiency and online marketing efforts fall to the manager who may lack the fundamental understandings of pixel metrics and how-to execution for SEO and SEM efforts.

With a person like Debbie at the helm, I suspect stores would more quickly gain proficiency and results in these critical pixel-driven efforts; and they'd likely lose less investment to trial and error, as well as losses due to lack of sufficient supervision and tracking of online and other marketing activities.

A single marketing department would offer other benefits such as the following:

- **More efficient allocation of resources.** It's not uncommon for used vehicle managers, Internet managers, and e-commerce directors to lament about the evenings they lose at home playing catch-up on tasks that Debbie might be better able to handle. I realize ours is a business where whiners are deemed losers, but some of the workloads and responsibilities strike me as unsustainable over the long haul. I think Debbie's help on such tasks would make for more clear-headed and satisfied managers at many stores. Their time and attention could be focused on helping Salesman Sam and Duane the Stocking and Pricing Guy become specialized experts at what they do. In turn, stores would see gains in CSI and repeat business as managers focus on improving and refining the processes that yield these benefits.

- **Consistent execution of marketing campaigns.** Much of the online marketing and pixel proficiency success that's been achieved at dealerships today has resulted from trial and error. This is not a bad thing, but Debbie would help stores build on what they've learned and establish more consistent processes, checklists, and performance standards to ensure more ROI-friendly tests of what works and doesn't.

- **Improved vendor ROI.** Debbie's knowledge of pixel proficiency and online marketing would help dealerships do a better job of evaluating the solutions the myriad of online marketing, SEO, and other pixel-minded vendors offer to stores. Today, many of the managers who make these decisions lack a fundamental understanding of how best to leverage their vendor relationships—a task that Debbie is more innately wired to do well.

ONLY THE FITTEST WILL SURVIVE

I've shared this three-department structure because I believe it offers a way to address the inefficiencies and dysfunction that exist in many stores as they try to transition their operations to meet the interests and needs of today's Internet-driven marketplace.

The fact that our industry has spent much of the past decade struggling to figure out how best to fit Internet-focused sales, inventory management, and marketing/merchandising into existing dealership department structures suggests a bolder, out-with-the-old/in-with-the-new approach may be in order.

This new structure may be a difficult pill for many dealers and used vehicle managers to swallow. I'll also concede that it may not work at some stores, where the current investment in Internet-driven processes has been a flat-out loser.

But even at these stores, I suspect the net profit returns on dealership operations still hover in the 1.5 to 2 percent range.

As expenses for people, facilities, and equipment continue to rise, the pressure on these margins will only grow. To me, the best way to mitigate these future profit pressures is to seek out the most efficient approaches to managing the processes and tasks necessary for success in today's more volatile, Internet-driven marketplace.

If nothing else, the three-department structure outlined here should at least spur conversations at dealerships to seek out the best way to position their people and processes for profitable, future-focused success.

A Peek into Dale's "Crystal Ball"

Anyone jumped into the car and made the trip to Blockbuster Video lately?

I can't remember the last time that happened in my family.

The fact is, we digitally record the movies we want to watch with TiVo, or Netflix sends them to us, or we go to *Hulu.com* to watch them. Nothing much has changed about our love for a good movie, but we sure have changed how we rent them.

I'm thinking of Blockbuster as I ponder the future of automotive retailing. To be sure, the business of renting videos is a far cry from selling cars.

But a closer examination of Blockbuster's current financial trouble and its struggle to adapt to the profound disruption the Internet has caused for the movie rental business reveals four telling similarities:

- **Significant overhead.** Blockbuster stores seemed to sprout in every bustling shopping center and strip mall across America. That was a foundational element of the company's early success: It knew how to pick its places.

  Now, Blockbuster is dismantling its empire. Against competitors who had considerably less invested in bricks and mortar, Blockbuster's retail footprint became a liability.

Dealers can't ditch their capital investments, but they can drive more performance and production from what they've built. This is the essence of velocity-minded management in used vehicles—doing more with less.

The dealers who remain in business as of this writing will shift from survive mode to thrive mode as they become more cost effective, efficient, and profitable in all they do.

- **An outdated business model.** Blockbuster failed to adapt quickly enough to the TiVos, Netflix, and Redboxes of the world. These more efficient and technology-enabled competitors found a way to offer the same movies cheaper, with more convenience and without late fees. They dialed into changing consumer preferences while Blockbuster maintained the status quo.

Traditional-minded dealerships now confront a similar quandary. They face more efficient and technology-powered competitors—including Texas Direct, CarMax, Auction Direct, and a growing number of velocity-minded dealers—who leverage these advantages to acquire and sell vehicles at a faster rate for less money and earn better returns on investment along the way.

- **Changing consumer loyalties.** Blockbuster saw huge success because it was largely the only game in town for many years. Its in-store movie selections were a big draw, and in-store customer associates were often knowledgeable and friendly. Late fees were a black eye for the company, but most customers accepted them as a consequence of their own inattention.

  Of course, these customers bolted in droves when offered the more convenient option of getting the same movies at home for less cost, without the hassle of late fees.

  Just like Blockbuster, franchised dealers enjoyed being the only game in town for their brands. That's still somewhat true for new vehicles, and far less true for used, with the exception of a handful of makes.

Today's vehicle buyers are like Blockbuster's former customers: They are quick to bail on a dealership that offers a less friendly process—from online to the showroom—when they find the vehicle they want to purchase. Inventory selection and price are top considerations, too, but it's the convenience, ease, and transparency of process that will turn a shopper into a buyer and repeat customer.

- **Pride of management.** Some studies of Block-buster suggest that the company's 10-year management team failed to see, and respond to, the threats that emerged from competitors like Netflix in as early as 1999. In 2007, the company brought in a new C-level team, but as recent reports indicate, the effort may turn out to be too little, too late[19].

A similar problem exists at many dealerships today. It's striking to visit dealers and used vehicle managers who at one time were "Kings of the Hill" in their markets: They are often the most reluctant to hear, let alone accept, that their declining sales volumes and deeper wholesale losses are a direct result of their *best* efforts to fix them.

It's difficult to tell guys who have been successful that the methods that drove their prior successes no

---

[19] http://www.scribd.com/doc/2621921/Blockbuster-Crisis-Management

longer fit a changed marketplace and, in fact, may be resulting in losing *future* business because they rub today's buyers the wrong way.

Unlike Blockbuster, however, today's dealers have an opportunity to catch the fall before it becomes fatal. They can start to have the conversations that eluded Blockbuster management for too long. They can begin to chart the transition to more customer-centric, efficient, and velocity-minded approaches to managing dealership operations.

I've intended this book to be part of this important transition. It's a bridge between dealers and used vehicle managers who have already come to terms with the realities of today's market and the more traditional stores that are struggling to understand what's hit them.

Velocity dealerships are the transition trailblazers. The stories they've kindly shared in this book offer important insights to guide all dealers and used vehicle managers toward more efficient and profitable Internet-focused organizations.

Not surprisingly, the Internet will continue to be the key change driver—starting with how car deals will go down in the not-so-distant future. The Internet will be a key cause of and solution to some of the challenges I see when I look into "Dale's Crystal Ball":

> *I have a saying—"documentation is the new negotiation." It conveys the idea that absolute transparency in deal-making, transforming it into real deal-making, will be paramount for sustained success at dealerships.*

Real Deal-Making. I have a saying—"documentation is the new negotiation." It conveys the idea that absolute transparency in deal-making, transforming it into real deal-making, will be paramount for sustained success at dealerships.

Think about the current flight of Carfax TV commercials. These commercials essentially tell today's dealer to "show me the Carfax."

Such are the expectations of today's buyers. They don't want to play deal-making games. In fact, most buyers despise them.

That's the opinion of Mark Rikess, CEO of The Rikess Group. He believes the preponderance of women and a younger generation of buyers, who want a fair deal without a hassle, indicates a shrinking percentage of buyers (30 percent, overall) with a thirst to negotiate a deal.

Interestingly, some velocity-minded managers are finding that a greater degree of transparency in their pricing and desking of deals results in customers *negotiating for less, if at all* when they buy.

This observation agrees with a study of deal-making transparency at Sam Swope Auto Group where salespeople shared real-time pricing information with consumers when they sat down to desk a deal. The test: How would customers react if salespeople addressed the group's Internet Value Pricing on a vehicle right up front?

Donovan says nearly 70 percent of customers at the test Cadillac store negotiated for less than $300 when salespeople explained the pricing approach up front, and shared a real-time view of online pricing and competitor comparisons to show supportive stats.

"We do it right up front in a proactive, not a defensive, way," Donovan says. "We have a lot more credibility and transparency."

The test results aren't surprising to Rikess, a pioneer in one-price selling who's developing sales models for limited negotiation-style deal-making.

"The interest in one-price and limited negotiation selling is growing," Rikess says. "It's a reflection of what today's customers are looking for."

To me, real deal-making isn't about one-price, but, rather, it's about transparency and showing the goods on a vehicle in ways many dealers have resisted for years. That's what private sellers do on *Craigslist*—they're wide open about the benefits and flaws of the vehicles they sell.

A Dealer Testifies

For some dealers, one-price selling fits their spiritual beliefs.

At a dinner one evening, velocity-minded dealer Chris Patton of the Mike Patton Auto Family, LaGrange Georgia, shared how and why he transitioned his stores to a one-price model.

It started while he was renewing his Christian faith, and applying it to how he does business. He ran across a Bible verse that hit home: the verse (Proverbs 20:10) says God dislikes "unequal weights and measures," Patton explains.

"I decided we needed to get away from negotiation, where we determined our pricing based on the customer, not the product. The switch to one-price was a core commitment on my part."

The transition hasn't been easy, but Patton views it as essential to meet his own needs and those of his customers.

Adjusting to this more transparent way of doing business, and adopting tools for in-store and online processes to address it, will be key challenges for all dealerships in the coming months and years. I predict some dealers like Swope will do even more to brand the real deal-style of doing business—akin to how labor groups implored consumers to "look for the union label[20]."

Dealership consultant George Gabriel offers another salient point on transparent sales processes

---

[20]http://unionsong.com/u103.html

and negotiation: The less transparency, the more a dealership is asking for negotiation. "The way dealers price cars, the way prices appear, and the way dealers present prices to customers are all designed to go for the big grosses," he says. "The way to get gross today is by not trying to get it."

Adam Simms of Toyota Sunnyvale agrees. His sales teams do not negotiate on used vehicle prices. Rather, they explain the store's market-based approach to pricing and use it to build value around a specific vehicle and its asking price. "Offering our car at the very best price up front seems to be a winner for the consumer and me," Simms says.

This breed of transparency also offers a variation on what Simms calls the old "take-away close."

"We'll do a consultation and show them the other vehicles they may want to consider if they don't buy our car," Simms says. "We'll note, of course, that our car might not be here when they come back."

Fierce competition from former franchised dealers. I received a note from a top-performing dealer who got the factory boot. He'd played by the rules, and leveraged his success with GM to buy a Chrysler store. His CSI, effective sales, and absorption rates were top tier. Yet, both factories pulled the rug out from under him. The investment he thought had built effectively went up in smoke. It pains me to relay his story. So what's he going to do?

Take a look and tell me this velocity dealer isn't going to grab some market share in both sales and service:

> "I have a passion for used cars and since I adopted velocity principles I have tremendous confidence in turning them. I will set a business plan for a used vehicle dealership that can offer maintenance service, tires, wheels, and details. I can use the service and detail area to feed the used business at a $20 less effective labor rate! I will take the best parts of both dealerships I lost, combine them into one tightly-run dealership, and start to enjoy life again. All this with no flooring, no control from manufacturer, no expense attributed to new vehicle sales, and best of all no more selling cars for little or no margin."

More Credit-Challenged Customers. Despite recent increases in the personal savings rate, the financial fundamentals for most consumer households remain weak. This will likely create a train wreck as dealers and used vehicle managers work with lenders who are reluctant to craft deals for customers with poor credit ratings and little cash to make down payments.

Of course, this will also create opportunities, particularly in the sub-prime arena. But even this business will prove more difficult to retain and keep.

Joe Orr at the Dick Hannah Dealerships says his group launched its own sub-prime financing company to address the virtual shutdown of lending to this sector of business.

Orr says the number of customers is almost too plentiful to handle. In addition, he calls the business challenging because the conditions the company uses to mitigate risk—like absolutely requiring job histories without lapses—are difficult for some customers to provide. "We don't sway from the guidelines at all," he says.

A related point: I should note that the velocity principles I've outlined in the book are not well suited for the sub-prime marketplace. The reason? Lenders have undue influence shaping the market. They control who qualifies for deals and the vehicles they can buy—effectively making the market. The lenders' role in sub-prime makes obtaining statistically valid reads on supply and demand metrics and trends nearly impossible.

The sub-prime lending marketplace appears to be loosening up, and I suspect the risk managers at finance companies will find a way to feed the marketplace's need for financing options that fit troubled household budgets.

I also wonder, however, if the credit-challenged nature of so many consumers may give rise to a completely different type of transaction—a hybrid that blends sub-prime financing with the time share-like vehicle use of Chicago's I-GO car-sharing program[21] or Zipcar. It's a far-out idea, but the seeds have been planted for this type of transportation purchase alternative to take shape.

Less Traditional Advertising. A shift is already happening at velocity dealerships where dealers and used vehicle managers have all but eliminated newspaper, radio, and TV advertising. Indeed, traditional advertising is often now focused on building the dealership brand and directing customers to check out convenient online shopping experiences.

Meanwhile, spending for online advertising—including investments in search-related marketing—will be a key focus for dealerships in the coming year. At Dick Hannah, Orr says the dealership's emphasis is on building positive online customer reviews and optimizing its web presence to capture consumers.

"Dealers need to take control of their own websites and online marketing," he says. "It's amazing to see what happens when you focus on this."

---

[21] http://www.igocars.org/   http://www.zipcar.com/

Ralph Paglia, head of digital marketing for ADP, agrees that dealers will increase their self-directed online marketing to attract customers, using browser cookie-based tactics like behavioral advertising that serves up ads when online shoppers visit non-automotive sites.

"We've flipped 180 degrees with online advertising and marketing," Paglia says. "Previously, dealers would buy leads and then advertise. Now they're advertising to drive more online consumers to their own inventories and websites, and then buying leads if they need them."

Shake-up in Third-Party Listing Sites. I'm told that *Google* is working on automotive pages that it hopes will rival those of *Cars.com* and *AutoTrader. com*. Dean Evans, chief marketing officer for *Dealer. com*, doesn't think *Google* will get in the business of listings, but it will continue to perfect its mission of serving up the most relevant content its algorithms believe consumers want to see. This offers opportunity for dealers, and it will put pressure on lead vendors to perform.

"*Google* want to bring their customers as close to the final product as possible, and not the middle man," Evans says.

Such discussions suggest that we'll see new opportunities for inventory listings and marketing that haven't existed to date.

Some evidence: In July 2009, *KBB.com* and *Vast. com, Inc.,* announced a partnership to deliver what they call The Trusted Marketplace for vehicle shoppers and dealerships. The companies believe dealers and used vehicle managers will respond to an inventory listing and lead generating platform that lets them set bids for the frequency and prominence of their vehicle listings that appear when consumers shop/search on *KBB.com.*

Vast's Benjamin Cohen says the pay-for-performance platform works similar to pay-per-click advertising on *Google* and other search engines. Advertisers bid for the frequency and placement of their ads to appear—thereby letting the market, rather than vendors, set the expense thresholds, he says.

So, dealers could dial up or dial down the advertising expenditures on a per-vehicle basis. The more they allocate, the more frequently and prominently their specific listings would appear. Cohen says the approach allows flexibility for dealers to address the needs of specific vehicles to drive leads and it gives them tools to monitor ROI on their spends.

"We see dealers increasing bids on older-age vehicles, just like they would spiff those cars on the physical lot," Cohen says.

To me, this signals that the world of online merchandising and marketing vendors for dealers is headed for what will likely be another level of pixel proficiency.

A Rise of Regional Mega-Dealers. There's an axiom in our business, "volume cures a lot of ills." Actually, the saying is more factually sound when restated as, "volume masks a lot of ills and leaves them for another day."

For many of the larger urban and suburban dealers, that day has arrived.

New vehicle sales at these stores are down, and used vehicle departments are not picking up enough of the slack—a struggle due to inefficient and traditional-minded processes for managing this side of the business.

Faced with revenue declines, these stores are struggling under the weight of expenses for buildings, land, inventory, people, and equipment that continue to rise. In some ways, these overhead costs are similar to the albatross of high health care and labor costs that squashed the ability of domestic automakers to refashion their businesses to meet a changing market. These large urban and suburban dealers also face more limited access to capital to re-shape their financial position. Such factors, coupled with resistance to adopt more efficient, velocity-minded processes and principles, are making it more difficult for these stores to survive, let alone thrive in today's more efficient and volatile marketplace.

While these stores grapple with problems akin to those at Blockbuster, a new breed of efficient and velocity dealers and used vehicle managers are rising up and claiming market share from the communities these larger dealers formerly served. These new regionally focused stores have innate cost and operational efficiencies that allow them to acquire market share and sell vehicles at margins that make no sense at the larger stores, given their innate inefficiencies and overhead.

These new regional players don't face the same cost pressures for buildings, land, equipment, and people that confront larger urban and suburban stores. What's more, they've become aggressive Internet retailers, allowing them to expand their target market areas and shift the historic balance of power that once favored larger competitors.

If I were an aspiring dealer today, I'd do what many manufacturing businesses have done: Search out the regions where population trends suggest growth and operational costs are far lower than the urban and suburban areas that once appeared as no-brainers for locating a new point.

More Creative Vehicle Sourcing. I've noted in previous chapters that I take issue with claims that there's a shortage of used vehicles. At the moment, the vehicles are available, but they're harder to find and acquire at prices that are right for a dealership, even for stores that adopt velocity management principles.

Used vehicle consultant Tommy Gibbs of Tommy Gibbs and Associates agrees. "The first thing dealers need to do is to quit listening to the propaganda that says they can't find used cars," he says. "The used cars are out there but dealers need an all-out assault on the marketplace in order to find them. More important is finding the ones that are going to turn the fastest."

That said, the past two years have seen far fewer new vehicles in factory production pipelines, and the outlook for the next two years is roughly similar to what we've already seen. New vehicle sales are not likely to surpass 14 million in the coming years. In addition, there are fewer leased vehicles in the current pipeline and rental fleets are holding their vehicles longer—although there are signs that leasing is picking up some steam.

These realities have led some dealers and used vehicle managers to predict a future shortage of used vehicles, potentially as early as 2011.

Will we see a used vehicle supply "shortage?"

The answer is yes in some price-sensitive segments of used vehicles. In the summer of 2009, the federal

Cash for Clunkers program has removed tens of thousands of older gas-guzzlers from used vehicle supplies—a trend that will add to sourcing pressures for dealers and used vehicle managers with low price lots that feature vehicles in the $3,000-$6,000 price range.

More broadly, market dynamics will make it more difficult for dealers and used vehicle managers to find and acquire prime late model vehicles. This may *feel* like a shortage but I predict dealers and used vehicle managers will devise creative solutions to feed their inventories. Programs like "We Pay Cash for Your Car" and buy-out offers in service lanes will gain in popularity as dealers and used vehicle managers hunt more diligently for viable inventory. At the same time, I expect velocity dealerships to hire inventory specialists like "Duane the Stocking and Pricing Guy" to help mine online sources more effectively for acquisitions.

The fact is, there will always be used vehicle buyers—and economic conditions suggest demand will only grow. The key for dealers and used vehicle managers will be establishing the processes that efficiently feed a science-like approach to inventory engineering to drive success in the coming years.

Technology-powered Pixel Oversight and Accountability. Most dealers and used vehicle managers rely on a variety of vendors to assist them with the tasks associated with pixel proficiency—from taking/uploading photos to handling the online marketing campaigns and SEO and SEM efforts. I expect more dealerships to hire people like "Digital Debbie" to bring these skills in-house, or to at least increase their own proficiency at overseeing these third-party efforts. It won't be long before technology gives Debbie and others more tools to do so.

Already, technology vendors are offering dashboards that distill, track, and audit the presentation of their vehicles on third-party and dealer-owned websites. This will go a step further, I believe, as technology allows one-stop audits of pixel processes and metrics—potentially even pixel proficiency scores to guide effective online merchandising and marketing.

With this technology, Debbie and other managers will be able to see where delays may occur in uploads of vehicles online or updates to key websites. Likewise, they'll see real-time feeds of online conversions and cost-per-lead data to better manage a store's pixel proficiency and online marketing efforts.

Overall, this is a good thing. It signals that pixel proficiency will gain greater attention and focus as dealers and used vehicle managers recognize their long-term success will be directly tied to how well they can execute efficiency-minded and technology-driven processes that enable them to truly become Internet Retailers.

A Critical Choice Awaits

My Crystal Ball predicts that the road ahead won't be an easy one, and, it's got plenty of potholes to throw the wheels of a dealership's operation out of alignment.

I do believe, however, that dealers and used vehicle managers who adopt velocity principles and shore up their paint and pixel proficiency will be the best positioned to see the potholes and avoid the bumpy ride that less market-attuned stores are likely to encounter.

It's not easy for dealers and used vehicle managers to adopt a velocity-minded approach for managing used vehicle operations. It takes guts, commitment, and fortitude to make what amounts to a dramatic departure from the traditional ways of doing business.

But given the road ahead, and the margin pressures that come with today's more efficient and volatile marketplace, dealerships face a make-or-break choice: Do we adopt newer, more efficient, profit-minded, and market-attuned ways of doing business or do we stick with tradition and hope for the best?

In the words of Bob Dylan, "The times they are a-changin'" and I say there's no time to waste. Which path will you choose?

INDEX

W

THE AUTHOR, DALE POLLAK

Dale Pollak is the Founder and Chairman of vAuto, Inc., named by *Inc. Magazine* as the second fastest growing software company in America in 2009. vAuto was established to help auto dealers improve the performance and profitability of their used vehicle departments.

Through its state-of-the-art technology, vAuto empowers dealers to appraise, stock, price and merchandise their used vehicles using real-time knowledge of marketplace supply, demand and price sensitivity trends. More than 2,500 franchised and independent dealerships, including five out of the six largest franchises of their respective brands, rely on the market-based metrics Pollak's innovative system provides to drive and fine tune their used vehicle operations.

For more information on vAuto and its product suite, visit www.vauto.com.

CPSIA information can be obtained at www.ICGtesting.com
225172LV00002BC/4/P

http://www.amazon.com

For detailed information about this and other orders, please visit Your Account. You can also print invoices, change your e–mail address and payment settings, alter your communication preferences, and much more – 24 hours a day – at http://www.amazon.com/your–account.

Returns Are Easy!

Visit http://www.amazon.com/returns to return any item – including gifts – in unopened or original condition within 30 days for a full refund (other restrictions apply). Please have your order ID ready.

Item Price	Total
$23.96	$23.96

Thanks for shopping at Amazon.com, and please come again!

Unless otherwise noted, items are sold by Amazon.com LLC and taxed if shipped to the states of Kansas, Kentucky, North Dakota, or Washington. For more tax and seller information, visit http://www.amazon.com/o/sor?o=102–7609794–9958643.

$23.96
$3.99
$27.95
$27.95
$0.00